PREVENTING
SPECIAL
EDUCATION

. . . for those who don't need it

Laurence M. Lieberman, Ed.D.

Laurence M. Lieberman
3/13/97

Library of Congress Catalogue Number 84-82152

Published by GloWorm Publications
70 Mount Vernon Street
Boston, Mass. 02108
617 624-0340

Printed in the U.S.A.
Nobb Hill Press, Inc.
Weston, Mass 02193

SUMMARY

ARTICLES

FOREWORD

The education of exceptional children is not wholly the responsibility of any one group of teachers. All educators and teachers have exceptional children under their care. The special class teacher usually has the extreme types of exceptional children — those that because of their handicaps or special abilities cannot be educated properly in the regular grades. The regular class teacher, on the other hand, has many children that are not mentally defective but are dull; children that are not markedly visually handicapped but have some visual defect; children that are not completely deaf but have some degree of impairment of hearing; children that are not delinquent but have minor behavior difficulties; children that are not gifted, but still are quite bright; and children that are not so crippled that they need special equipment, yet have minor physical handicaps. In other words the regular classroom teacher has in her class not only so-called average children, but many that possess minor handicaps or special abilities. Every teacher, therefore, is to some extent a teacher of exceptional children, and should utilize with some modifications the techniques employed to educate the more extreme form of handicapped or gifted children.

It is hoped that in the future, all special class teachers will contribute their knowledge and special skill to the regular classroom teacher who has always had, and probably will always have, many minor forms of exceptional children in her classroom.

Samuel A. Kirk
Journal of Exceptional Children
November, 1941

Public Law 94-142 was passed with a very clear mandate for the handicapped. When this mandate was given, a handicapped child was not handicapped because he was failing in school; he was failing in school because he was handicapped.

Laurence M. Lieberman
The Implications of Non-Categorical Special Education. <u>Journal</u> of <u>Learning</u> <u>Disabilities</u>, Feb. 1980, Vol. 13, No. 2.

INTRODUCTION

The propositions contained in this guide have evolved over ten years. Some were part of a 1971 keynote presentation entitled, "The State of the Art of Learning Disabilities." As Special Education underwent its unique changes through the 1970's, the presentation became "Mainstreaming: Strategy or Tragedy?" Ideas were added and subtracted. Some were expanded while others became a satire on the educational establishment.

The thread of a philosophical statement began to appear as the title changed to "Quality Education for All Children." In the relatively recent past, the presentation took a practical turn in emphasis and for a large audience of school superintendents became, "How to Reduce Special Education Costs."

The guide should be considered in its totality. However, an all or nothing approach would provide no useful purpose for educational decision-makers. Each proposition should be thought of as a possible program strategy that might benefit some component of the educational system, without necessarily compromising others. They are not presented in hierarchical order. Each one makes a contribution to the overall theme. Each school system should consider these propositions within its own context.

The title, "Preventing Special Education . . . for those who don't need it," is the clearest possible statement of the purpose of this guide. Current educational research and literature is replete with references to overkill in every facet of special education service delivery: referrals, testing, programming, conferencing, paperwork, diagnosing, labeling, and above all, promoting special education as the means by which regular education problems are solved.

Second only to this is the contention by many associated with education, that the vast majority of children having school based problems do not have anything inherently wrong with them. These two premises lead to the following conclusions:

a. Both special education and regular education are contributing to the expansion of special education beyond its presumed focus, which is handicapped children.

b. Financial cost and human cost, such as blaming the student and stigmatizing him, is outstripping any perceived positive result of the proliferation of special programs for children with school based problems.

c. When a student fails, the system fails. Yet the system persists in the counterproductive activity of seeking student change, while neglecting system change.

d. The educational system is responsible for creating many of its own failures and only it holds the key to preventing these failures.

e. The most efficient, cost-effective, and potentially beneficial approach to problem solving in education is to identify and eliminate counterproductive practices, rather than trying to solve the problems caused by these practices.

In time, the emphasis will change. There will always be new ideas, new values, and most assuredly, new bandwagons. There will also be old methods in new packages. One central theme will always remain. Schools exist for children. Educators must obligate themselves to children, which means forever being at the razor's edge of determining positive, life enhancing practices, and excising negative, destructive ones.

Laurence M. Lieberman, Ed.D
September 9, 1984

I. REGULAR EDUCATION PROGRAM PROPOSITIONS

A. Generate awareness on the part of regular education teachers and administrators that they have responsibility for all students assigned to them, regardless of time out for special education services.

Over the last five to ten years, special education programs have undergone a phenomenal growth process. During this same period of time, regular education has experienced severe cutbacks in the form of budget cuts and growth ceilings, school closings, disappearing extra-curricular activities, and the loss of personnel such as librarians, and music and art teachers. Even core curriculum teachers have lost jobs, with the immediate consequence of larger class size for those who remain.

One of the most effective, yet simple ways to provide this information is through the presentation of data. Everyone has experienced the growth of special education while regular education has tried to hold the line against program losses, but few school personnel have generated the actual data that would serve to concretize the experience. The primary purpose of this data collection would be to promote awareness on the part of regular educators. The appropriateness of the data and the format for presentation should suit its purpose. If this is not carefully thought out, special education could be subjected to a severe and unwarranted backlash.

For example, regular education teachers believe that special education teachers have easier jobs. It is very difficult to establish cooperative relationships on behalf of children in a climate of jealousy. The major contention seems to be that special education teachers have responsibility for fewer children at a time, if not overall. A further notion is that these teachers have greater time flexibility. Other considerations may be that they have no bus duty or that they are not directly answerable to the Principal. Sometimes this is all true. Many times it is not. In addition to resource room caseloads that exceed regular education classes, most of the work is individualized in such a way as to keep special education teachers continuously engaged in student interaction. They must be fully aware of each child's curriculum, objectives, strategies, materials, rate of learning, rate of progress, and major problems. They are always being torn between their own objectives and those of the classroom teacher. Scheduling is a nightmare. Children are marching in and out all day, and with non-categorical and cross-categorical programming, the range in both age and handicap can be immense. Special education teachers must be master diplomats and calm negotiators. All this is generally unknown to classroom teachers.

Although awareness and responsiblity may be the purpose, the spin-off objective is to have the regular education staff begin to analyze their functioning and how it may be contributing to cutbacks such as loss of planning time, materials, etc. It will not be necessary to suggest that these conditions are undesirable. Classroom teachers will draw their own conclusions. The administrative role is to run interference between the impulse to derogate special education and the valid alternative of examining one's own contributory behavior.

Providing data and having teachers draw their own conclusions is an indirect, inductive method to generating regular education responsibility for children with problems. It may be preferable to the direct approach, which is to tell them. However, both strategies have their place. It is undoubtedly true that some people need to be told in very direct words. An example might be, "No matter how much time a child spends in special services, when he is programmed into your room, you are responsible for his curriculum and instruction and grades and all aspects of his schooling pertaining to that class time."

A further formalizing step geared to generating responsibility would be to include in the Individualized Education Plan (IEP) the modifications and accomodations that must be made on behalf of the child in regular class settings. The question is not remediation versus compensation. The question is who does which. Special education teachers should work on deficits or weaknesses and attempt to raise the level of competency to an acceptable functional level. Regular education teachers should allow for compensation and let children work around their problems. For every child in need of special education services, not one, but two conceptually different plans are required. In fact, it is not so much two plans as two sets of strategies that must be developed. The compensatory changes required in regular class settings could be a one page addendum to the IEP. If these changes are presented as suggestions, they may serve little purpose. Unfortunately, the more formal the language (e.g., modifications rather than suggestions for modifications), the better the results.

The first step is awareness. Yet, awareness cannot be considered along a continuum that begins and ends. It is part of all thought. Awareness does not lead to attitude change, which does not lead to changes in teaching. The line flows in every direction simultaneously. The remaining parts of this guide all impact on these fundamental concerns.

B. Create the understanding that there are direct links between regular classroom teachers over-referring students to special education and regular education being stripped of programs, teachers, and administrators.

This is fairly obvious to those who already understand it. To those who don't, it seems to be a mystery that cannot be unlocked by just saying it. Merely telling teachers that over-referral to special education could result in the growth of special education programs at the expense of regular education is clearly not enough. Somehow the fact that school system money is finite and can only be distributed in different ways escapes many classroom teachers. A primary consideration is the realization that over-referral may be an indictment of the teacher and/or the curriculum.

Again, hard data must be collected and presented; data that indicates dollars spent for out of classroom time that could be spent in other ways. Facts and figures usually confound even the most obstinate teachers who refuse to see the realities of this process. Although the figure will vary, ten percent of the students, kindergarten through high school, receiving some form of special education services (including speech) seems to be accepted by many school systems. One would expect this figure to vary upward in inner city schools and downward in suburban schools. This expectation may or may not be valid, as the proliferation of special education services in the suburbs may far exceed those of urban areas. Nevertheless, ten percent seems to be an acceptable program figure, as well as an epidemiological statistic of the incidence of handicapping conditions among children in America. Applying this percentage to each classroom in the country would seem logical. The microcosm should reflect the major significant elements of the macrocosm.

Hypothetically, ten percent of the children in any given classroom might be designated as having some handicapping condition and be in need of special education services. This figure will vary, but there is a referral point, beyond which a monitoring and examination system should go into effect. This point is arbitrary, although a twenty percent referral rate for classes of twenty-five or more seems to be a reasonable limit.

Monitoring and examination may begin with a perusal of the referral forms and a determination of the status of those students referred. This raises the entire question of whether special education services are appropriate for a particular child, which in turn, would validate the original referral. Both the appropriateness of the referral and the determination that the child is in need of special education services must be fully scrutinized. This will be addressed later in this guide.

The assumption is that occasionally, twenty percent of a given class should be referred and may require special education services, but it is usually too high to be a valid indication of the incidence of handicapped children in need of special education. Upon examining the records, especially the referral forms, a pattern may emerge that speaks more to a particular teacher's weakness than it does to the nature of handicapped children. This might be ad-

dressed by a special education administrator and the building Principal, to help the teacher examine his or her own
strengths and weaknesses and develop a plan for in-service,
that might include in-class consultation with a peer, special education teacher, and/or psychologist.

This process should be used to concretize the fact
that teachers seem to know intuitively, who among them
are effective and ineffective with certain kinds of children. This is accomplished through noting teacher referral
patterns over time and acting accordingly. The implication is for highly specific in-service training rather than
random in-service training, which is another subsequent
topic.

C. Effect a teacher-child match.

This is at the cutting edge of the intent of this guide. It speaks directly to the fact that under least restrictive environment guidelines, regular education should exercise all its options prior to the advent of special education services. When children and teachers are matched effectively, special education is appropriately conceptualized and regular education takes a giant step toward solving its own problems.

The teacher-child match may take place on many levels. Teachers and children can be matched across continuums of:

1. instructional style and learning style

2. teacher personality variables and learner personality variables

3. teacher behavior management strategies and learner responses to different management strategies

4. teacher classroom organization and learner needs for certain organizational styles

5. etc., etc.

The list is endless and so are the combinations of variables. The books written on instruction, personality, learning, and behavior fill entire libraries.

The way to avoid being overwhelmed and rendered helpless is to recognize that an in-depth analysis of these factors in either the teacher or the student is seldom, if ever, necessary. Everyone seems to know whether or not education is working effectively for both teacher and child. Admittedly, this is an anti-analytic position, condoning subjectivity and intuition as being equal to or more important than objectivity in these circumstances. Given the realities of time and the effort required, it is much more practical to consider the gestalt view, which is the whole being much more than the sum of the parts.

The teacher selection process is a major, critical component of preventing special education for those who don't need it. It could be one of the most important activities conducted on behalf of children in all of education. The teachers know themselves and each other. They also know the children. At the end of each year, they must be given the opportunity to help select which teacher receives which child the following year. Some teachers are very good at dealing with certain kinds of learning and behavior problem children. Placing a child with a particular teacher can mean the difference between a miserable year or a productive one. It can also mean the difference between a special education referral and a regular education problem resolution. The major difficulty associated with this strategy is that those teachers who are recognized as effective with problem children usually end up with many of them. Educators must recognize this phenomenon and plan accordingly. Those teachers selected to teach specific problem children should have added support from consultants and administrators. They should also be able to negotiate class size. If four problem children are to be placed in one classroom, let eight other so-called normal children be placed elsewhere. In other words, these teachers should have smaller class sizes, with the result that their colleagues will have larger ones than what the average would be. This should be addressed openly with the staff, so that it is agreed upon and shown that there can be a reward for being willing and able to deal with problem children. Also, after a sequence of two or three difficult years, those teachers should have a respite year of minimally difficult children in their classrooms. This is a precaution against burn-out.

The reason for emphasizing the selection process should be quite evident to most administrators, especially Principals. It seems that once the selection of a classroom teacher is made and the school year begins, it is almost impossible to convince a Principal to change a child's regular classroom teacher. Principals, like teachers, are on a continuum ranging from being open and flexible to being completely rigid and unchanging. However, it seems that changing a child's teacher pushes even flexible Principals to the other end of the continuum. It does happen, but usually the child makes the decision. He returns home crying every day and refuses to go to school each morning. Ultimately the parent comes to school and accuses the teacher of destroying his or her child. Then, the Principal might make the needed change. Unfortunately, teachers generally do not go to the Principal and say that a very bad match exists and that all interests would best be served by a change.

The two reasons that Principals give for not subscribing to this strategy are ludicrous and scary, respectively. The first reason is that if one did it, everyone would want to do it. If this ever really happened (to my knowledge, it never has), it might be acceptable grounds to fire that teacher. Also, this process is to be based on sound reasoning and evidence, not whimsy. When a Principal invokes this message, who is he thinking of, himself or the child?

The second reason is frightening indeed. "The child has to learn how to live with adversity." An adult would never allow himself to be forced (if he could help it) into a destructive situation, every day, six hours a day, for an entire year. A child does not have the coping mechanisms of an adult. The only possible results from such a circumstance are an emotionally disturbed child and a child who is permanently turned off to school. Being miserable in school every day is not the enlightened path to building character. It is the darkened path to a character disorder.

D. Establish a stringent pre-referral process and problem solving teams.

This is a critical element of the special-regular education process that was neglected in P.L. 94-142 and most state legislation. In order for the system to function in line with its conceptualization, a series of steps must be undertaken prior to the advent of special education services.

The most significant implication of least restrictive environment thinking and mainstreaming in general is seldom addressed; the idea that full time placement in a regular classroom is the most, least restrictive environment and therefore, regular education should try every option available to it prior to implementing special education procedures. Theoretically, all attempts made to maintain the child as a full participant in regular education are part of the pre-referral process. Some of these major attempts will be addressed in subsequent parts of this guide. At this point, suffice it to say that special educators and ancillary professionals do very costly evaluations which result in recommendations that should and could have been implemented prior to the evaluation. It is fairly obvious that the major reason for testing is professional credibility. Unfortunately, few educators and parents will accept ideas when they spring from minds instead of formal test protocols.

The steps in the pre-referral process usually begin with a perceived problem. At the beginning stage, ownership of the problem is still not claimed, nor should it be.

As soon as the referral becomes a reality, the emphasis shifts almost totally in the direction of the child owning the problem. Therefore, the beginning is a critical time, when teachers are more amenable to self-examination, introspection, and a willingness to accept interactive responsibility.

The process may begin with a pre-referral form that outlines the child's apparent difficulties, his status in the class, his informally assessed learning and behavioral style, and the attempts made by the teacher to correct the problems. Formalizing the process in and of itself may reduce referrals. It seems that when teachers have to put something in writing, they tend to mobilize themselves to correct the problem and not be so hasty in terms of sending for the special education cavalry. Of course one would not want the process or the form to be so demanding as to create an under-referral problem. In other words, having the child in the classroom and not telling anyone that he is experiencing great difficulty is to be equally avoided.

With children being taught by so many different teachers, the form should be contributed to and signed by all the teachers having responsibility for the particular student. This promotes consensus of opinion, helps to rule out personality conflicts as the sole source of difficulty, and promotes problem solving behavior.

The pre-referral form is submitted to the building level pre-referral committee. This group should not necessarily be different from a regular education problem solving team. In fact, it makes sense to have this committee conceptually established as a problem solving team. The team can operate in a far different manner from being restricted to a decision of allowing the process to continue, or preventing the referral from proceeding further (it rarely stops the process, unless the Special Education Director happens to be sitting in on the meeting).

It seems incredible but true that it took special education legislation, IEP's, due process, and tons of forms and paperwork in order for educators to realize that they could sit together with each other, and with professionals from other disciplines, to make decisions and attempt to work out solutions to children's problems. One of the single most important aspects of the pre-referral process, is to recognize the fact that teachers can solve problems they are having with children and that providing a forum in the form of a problem solving team is a major step toward generating and implementing strategies on behalf of these children. An excellent model for regular education problem solving teams has been developed by Dr. James Chalfant of the University of Arizona and Dr. Margaret Van Dusen Pysh, Northern Suburban Special Education District, Highland Park, Illinois. (See the Learning Disabilities Quarterly, Volume 2, Summer, 1979. "Teacher Assistance Teams: A Model for Within-Building Problem Solving." Also, a November, 1981 Counterpoint article is reproduced in this guide.)

It takes commitment and time. It might require staying in school until 5:00 P.M. one or two days a week. It might mean occasionally meeting with colleagues informally on weekends for one or two hours. What it really means is a willingness to do what needs to be done in order to make the process of education a life enhancing force for both children and adults.

The team should be composed primarily of regular education teachers. It is important that someone in authority be present, such as the Principal, who can help make program decisions on an immediate basis. It should follow an empirical or research paradigm. A problem is specified by a referring teacher. It is discussed and hypotheses are generating regarding causes of the problem and potential solutions. Specific strategies are laid out in accordance with the teacher's responsiblities and those of ancillary personnel, the role of consultation and support, daily and/or weekly reporting procedures, parental involvement, objectives and time lines. An implementation phase is begun that may take as long as one or two months. Monitoring and interim evaluation may take place weekly. An evaluation plan is set up in such a way as to provide a relatively easy decision at the end of the process. The problem solving team should be programming for success. However, a major function should be to decide whether or not to continue with the special education process. A regular classroom teacher's inability to deal effectively with a child or certain children should not be perceived as failure; especially after the problem solving team has exhausted its capabilities. It is an important step in ascertaining real handicapping conditions and gives greater credence to a long term commitment as opposed to a quick fix approach.

TEACHER ASSISTANCE TEAMS
A Model For Within–Building Problem Solving

by James C. Chalfant and
Margaret Van Dusen Pysh

The Teacher Assistance Team (TAT) is a system for within-building problem-solving by and for regular classroom teachers. It is based on the belief that, if they work together in a problem-solving process, teachers can develop the skills and knowledge to teach many students with learning and behavior problems.

The system is designed to provide prompt, accessible support to teachers. Teachers refer students with problems to a team of three elected teachers within the building. The team and the referring teacher jointly engage in a structured process of conceptualizing the problem, brainstorming solutions, and planning interventions. Parents, students, and other specialists participate in some cases. Follow-up meetings are held to evaluate the student's progress and to plan further intervention. When appropriate, students are referred to special education.

The model is quite cost-effective. It has been designed to minimize time and paperwork, and no additional staff need be hired. It has been shown to be effective in a wide variety of school districts, ranging from metropolitan to rural. To date, the Teacher Assistance Team model has been implemented in ten states and in four provinces of Canada.

The original concept and teams were established with the guidance and support of Kenneth Crowell, former Superintendent, and Robert Moultrie, former Pupil Personnel Director, in District 108, Highland Park, Illinois. The model was further developed and evaluated in Arizona, Nebraska, and Illinois from 1978 to 1980 under a grant from the Office of Special Education's Division of Personnel Preparation. The full final report from that project is available from the developer. The results are summarized below as four claims of the program, i.e., Teacher Assistance Teams:

1. Help teachers to establish successful programs for students with learning and behavioral problems;

2. Provide support to teachers in mainstreaming handicapped students;

3. Provide an efficient pre-referral screening for special education services; and

4. Can be effectively replicated in school districts with a variety of characteristics.

These teams should not be confused with the building level pre-referral screening teams of multi-disciplinary teams composed of specialists, such as psychologists, social workers, guidance counselors, remedial reading teachers, and special education teachers. Teacher Assistance Teams differ in membership, rationale, and responsibilities. Composed of regular teachers, not specialists, teams' major responsibility is to assist regular classroom teachers in individualizing instruction to meet the needs of any child — normal, gifted, or handicapped — not simply to reduce referral rate (which TAT does) nor to satisfy state and federal regulations with respect to identification, screening, or diagnosis. The primary focus is on helping fellow teachers resolve problems in their classrooms.

Assumptions

This model is based on four assumptions: (a) regular education teachers have the skills and knowledge to help many students with learning and behavior problems; (b) teachers can resolve more problems working together than alone; (c) regular education should make every effort to resolve problems at the building level before referring a child to special education and labeling him handicapped; and (d) teachers learn best by doing; the best way to increase their skills is by helping them to solve immediate problems in their classrooms.

Operating Procedures

Flexibility is one of the major strengths of the Teacher Assistance Model. The staff of each building has the flexibility to develop operating procedures which are most compatible with the organizational structure, staff composition, and interpersonal dynamics of the group. Figure 1 portrays how the majority of the teams tend to function.

Teacher Referral. A teacher who is having difficulty teaching a child with learning or behavior problems submits a short summary of observations of the child. The summary consists of: (a) a description of the performance desired of the child; (b) a list of the student's strengths and weaknesses; (c) a description of what the teacher has already done to resolve the problem; and (d) any relevant background information and test results.

An analysis of the kinds and frequency of problems found among the 200 children who were referred to TAT by regular teachers at the 15 demonstration sites revealed 18 major problem areas (see Table 1). The children who were referred averaged nearly five problem areas per child. It should be noted that the kinds and frequency of problems brought to TAT's change over time. Initially, teachers seem to seek assistance with classroom management problems, such as work habits and inappropriate behaviors of children. As teachers become more proficient in coping with these problems, however, referrals begin to reflect a need for assistance in teaching academic skills. Requests for assistance in improving children's learning styles, thinking, reasoning, and memory seem to increase when teachers have gained confidence and have achieved success in teaching basic academic skills.

Reviews of Referrals. The team coordinator reviews the referring teacher's summary to ensure that it includes the necessary information. Team members are alerted and asked to read the referral, identify problem areas, study their interrelationship, and consider possible recommendations for the meeting. (Team members learn a simple graphic method of analyzing problems.) As much information as possible should be shared and reviewed before the meeting. This reduces the need for oral reviews and summaries and allows team members to devote meeting time to solving problems.

Requests for Specific Information. After reviewing the referral, it may be necessary for the coordinator to talk with the teacher to clarify certain statements on the referral or to obtain additional information.

Classroom Visits. It is sometimes helpful for one of the team members to visit the classroom and observe the child. In some instances, the Principal can take over a team member's class for 15 to 20 minutes while he or she conducts the observation, or another teacher might take the observing teacher's class for a time. Having one of the team members observe may yield additional insights into the problem, as well as give the referring teacher an ally during the team meeting.

Problem-Solving Meeting: The TAT meeting lasts for 30 minutes and includes the following steps: (a) reach consensus about the nature of the problem; (b) negotiate one or two objectives with the referring teacher; objectives should be in terms of the behaviors the child should achieve; (d) select the methods the referring teacher would like to try; the team defines the methods; (e) fix responsibility for carrying out the recommendations (who, what, when, where, why, how); and (f) establish a follow-up plan for continued support and evaluation.

Training is necessary for teachers to accomplish all six stages of the meeting in 30 minutes. By using good communication principles and applying group dynamics, most teams have no difficulty staying within the 30-minute time frame.

Recommendations. The end product of the TAT meeting should be: (a) specific recommendations for individualizing instruction for the child; (b) recommendations for informal assessment by the child's teacher or team member; or (c) referral for special help.

Time and Paperwork

Typically, teams meet once a week for one hour or twice a week for 30 minutes. During peak referral times, more time may be required. One team can usually serve 20 to 40 students during a year with continuing follow-up. Each team member can expect to spend no more than a one-hour meeting and half hour in preparation each week. Duty on TAT should be in lieu of another duty, such as playground, bus, or lunchroom duty.

Paperwork is minimal. The referring teacher compiles the summary observation form, which takes about 15 minutes. An instructional recommendation form, including objectives, methods and evaluation, is completed during the meeting, with a carbon copy. No paperwork is done outside the meeting and no clerical support is required.

Advantages of TAT

The Teacher Assistance Team model has advantages for regular teachers, administrators, special education, and students and parents.

For regular teachers, TAT provides support for individualizing instruction: increases teacher skill and comfort level in dealing with children who have special needs; makes possible immediate response to classroom needs; suppies 3-on-1 inservice; shares teacher competencies within the building; and generalized interventions to other children in the class.

For administrators, TAT shifts staff concern to positive, constructive problem-solving; utilized staff members more effectively; improves staff communication and skill; saves time and money by reducing referrals to special education; and is cost-effective.

For special education, TAT provides an efficient pre-referral screening for special education services, thereby reducing inappropriate referrals; assists in providing support to mainstreamed handicapped students; and allows special education to focus its resources on the truly handicapped students.

For students and parents, TAT provides an alternative for slow learners and children not eligible for special education services; includes parents in planning before referral to special education; gives students immediate intervention; and gives students the opportunity to sit on the team and take responsibility for their own behavior.

Table 1
Reasons for Referral to TAT

Problems	Frequency
Work Habits	179
Classroom Behavior	115
Interpersonal Behavior	112
Reading	90
Attention	78
Printing and Writing	55
Expressive Language	45
Memory	44
Arithmetic	42
Spelling	37
Self-Concept	33
Emotional Problems	31
Perceptive Language	26
Discrimination of Symbols	24
Physical Problems	22
Motor Performance	22
Speech	8
Reasoning	7

For futher information, contact JAMES CHALFANT, Professor, Department of Special Education, Education Building, University of Arizona, Tucson, Arizona 87521; (602) 626-3248; or MARGARET PYSH, Northern Suburban Special Education District, 760 Red Oak Lane, Highland Park, Illinois; (312) 831-5100.

E. Recognize that standardized achievement testing may be a prime contributor to the inordinate growth of special education.

Standardized achievement testing is a business. Test publishers have one goal; to make money. Vast amounts of money for achievement testing is set aside in school budgets each year. The return of something of value is suspect. Yet, the test publishers are not necessarily at fault. "Let the buyer beware" should be a familiar slogan. Sometimes education's foolish consumerism makes it its own worst enemy. More likely than not it is local school board politics and an uneducated community that gives rise to such things. The power of politics and ignorance can, and does, override all of the following:

1. The validity and reliability of the tests themselves are always problematic.

2. Standardized testing procedures are always at risk from system to system, school to school, and even classroom to classroom.

3. Group testing always has a standard error of measurement that is far greater than individual testing. A great deal of accuracy is compromised.

4. Some school systems have automatic special education referral policies for those children scoring below a certain point on the test.

5. Administering these tests to certain children will create an orientation toward the child owning the problem and in fact being handicapped, which is the antithesis of what this guide stands for.

6. Ceiling scores are not valid indications of true ability. Some tests suggest that a child can read at a twelfth grade level when he has passed all items that reflect a seventh or eighth grade level.

7. In April, 1981, the Delegates Assembly at the International Reading Association's annual meeting adopted the following resolution: "The IRA strongly advocates that those who administer standardized reading tests abandon the practice of using grade equivalents to report performance of either individuals or groups of test takers."

8. Because the test data is at risk, all educational assumptions based on the test data are at risk. That includes program placement, materials, strategies, etc.

9. Due to the expenditure of funds and the games school politicians play with numbers such as national averages and community standing, the test publishers are actually dictating curriculum content. Sometimes pressured teachers teach directly to the test. A parent who is told that his child scored poorly on a particular subpart because it wasn't covered in class will want to know why. That parent will not necessarily accept a response that suggests the test publisher has no a priori right to dictate what that child should or should not be learning. All the parent may care about is that he has a child with a low score and the teacher did not fulfill his or her obligation to the child.

Reflecting on these test related issues in the context of special education and handicapped children can be overwhelming. However, if school system personnel believe that standardized achievement testing is important and necessary, special provisions must be made for handicapped children regarding the taking, scoring, and meaning of these tests. Here are some available options:

1. The test is read to the student.

2. The test is administered untimed.

3. The test is administered twice.
    a. The student does it on his own.
    b. The test is read to the student.

4. The test is administered individually or in a small group.

5. The student practices how to take the test.

6. The student writes in the booklet instead of using the answer sheet.

7. The student takes a lower form of the test.

The choices should reflect a policy that doing poorly on the test does not constitute a handicapping condition, nor is it grounds for special education. Furthermore, the options listed above should be written into the IEP's of those children who have already been determined to be handicapped and in need of special education.

F. **Understand that retention (grade repetition) does not solve the long term problems of handicapped children.**

Some school systems use retention in place of special education. Sometimes retention is even used as punishment or as the "Sword of Damocles," hanging over the head of the child.

A distinction must be made between retention and non-promotion. Retention is a potential, program enhancing regular education option, chosen on behalf of a child. It occurs primarily in the elementray school and especially during the years of kindergarten through second grade. Non-promotion is a secondary school phenomenon and should be thought of as a potential result of a student not meeting pre-set standards. Although retention and non-promotion both result in grade repetition, their purposes and implications for the educational future of the student are completely different.

The research on retention says essentially two things; it works to the benefit of children and it works to the detriment of children. An equal number of articles can be found for it and against it. All the research studies that address the efficacy of retention as a positive influence on students, maintain one major conclusion; retention, if it works for the student, does not work by itself. It requires something in addition to just grade repetition and that something else is usually some form of special education services.

For most handicapped children, retention at best forestalls the inevitable, which is many years of long, hard work. It adds the possibility of one or more years of pursuing that work. At worst, retention gives a false sense of doing something positive, while possibly being extremely debilitating. For a full explanation of the basis on which a retention decision should be made, see my article entitled "A Decision-Making Model For In-Grade Retention," Journal of Learning Disabilities, May, 1980, Vol. 13, No. 5.

A DECISION-MAKING MODEL FOR IN-GRADE RETENTION (NONPROMOTION)

Laurence M. Lieberman, EdD

Research on retention (also known as in-grade repetition or nonpromotion) is inconclusive to date. There are as many studies for it as against it with some highly questionable research methodologies on both sides. Disregarding the research, to make a decision for or against retention on the basis of statistical evidence rather than on an in-depth analysis of all factors contributing to each individual situation seems foolhardy.

The decision-making model that follows is one of rational problem solving. Four categories for each factor are possible: for retention, against retention, undecided (evidence weighted equally for and against), and not applicable. The factors themselves are not weighted because it is the individual student who must give weight to the factors. For example, a second grader may be so large as to establish physical size as a critical factor well beyond its meaning for an average size second grader.

CHILD FACTORS

Physical Disabilities
Children who suffer from cerebral palsy, deafness, blindness, congenital heart defects, arthritis, and other physical abnormalities may demonstrate limited readiness skills, poor language development, and deficient knowledge or awareness of their surroundings caused by limited experience.

Physical Size
Size may be considered in terms of small, medium, and large. Obviously, small stature would be associated with "for retention," while largeness

would tend to mitigate against it. In extremes of very small and very large, physical size takes on important value.

Academic Potential

Potential is defined in terms of learning rate, which may range from better than appropriate to appropriate to slow to the point of continuous, compounded under-achievement. The distinction to be made here is between chronic under-achievement (which should not necessarily be a criterion for retention) and the need for prolonged periods of practice when preliminary learning takes place (which may be a criterion for retention). A distinction should also be made between those students assessed as having more permanent slow-learning attributes and those who exhibit behaviors suggesting that their slow learning is temporary. In the former case, special education may be warranted apart from retention considerations. The latter case suggests a "for retention" factor.

Psychosocial Maturity

An indication that psychosocial maturity should be a factor in a "for retention" decision often comes from a description of the child as being a "baby" by either his parents or teacher. The behaviors associated with this term are most often normal in younger children — e.g., thumbsucking, inability to delay gratification, inability to take turns, inability to attend for more than a few minutes at a time, and a demonstrably greater interest in all forms of play and fantasy activities.

On the opposing side some children are described as "little old men and women." These children give a strong impression that they are able to fend for themselves in an independent manner and seem to engage adults in adult-level social repartee. They are not so much well adjusted as adjusted to an adult world. Sometimes these children have difficulty in relating to peers. Certainly the psychosocial maturity continuum is broad, and there is an infinite number of points between extremes.

Neurological Maturity

Again this is a situation in which behaviors considered normal in younger children are persistently manifested in older youngsters. Immature behaviors generally fall into one or more of the following conditions: hyperactivity, gross motor deficits, fine motor coordination difficulties, language and articulation problems, distractibility, short attention span, and many different types of perceptual disturbances. The lack of establishment of handedness and other confusions associated with body awareness and movement also contribute to what is considered to be neurological immaturity. This factor is especially significant for educational practices because it directly challenges chronological age, which is the deciding factor in initial grade placement.

It is apparent that neurological maturity deserves an extremely important consideration in school entry. Many retentions are corrective measures for school intake based solely on chronological age.

Child's Self-Concept

For purposes of making a decision for or against retention, self-concept is primarily considered in terms of self-esteem. This involves the child's values and judgment of his own goodness, badness, or worth. A major question in the decision-making process is the impact of retention on the child's self-concept. The concern is the possibility of detrimental impact when the child becomes convinced that he is looked upon as a failure.

Depending on grade placement, this problem is often more difficult for the adults involved with the child than for the child himself. Children at certain ages seem far more adaptable to retention than they are credited. However, many factors have bearing on this point. The important questions seem to be

1. If the child has a good self-concept, will retention debilitate him and give him a long-lasting, low self-concept?

2. If the child has a low self-concept, will retention debilitate him further to the point of consigning him to a school career fraught with misery?

3. If the child has a low self-concept, is it the result of low achievement, and will retention foster his achievement, which will in turn, enhance his self-concept?

A popular misconception should not be overlooked in trying to answer these questions. Students, by virtue of retention, do not automatically go to the top of the class in the repeated grade. More often they enter somewhere in the middle.

Child's Ability to Function Independently

This factor is highly significant because as children progress through the grades, greater and greater responsibility for independent learning and performance is expected. When a child requires constant supervision to maintain attention, to exhibit appropriate behavior, to be task oriented, and to perform the dictates of the task correctly, he may be high risk for satisfactory school learning. Motivation as a volitional quality is not considered here. A willful lack of task performance is almost never used as a factor in retention because the retention may represent disciplinary action, which is considered to be highly inappropriate. It is likely that children who need constant supervision as the result of physical, cognitive, or emotional factors or all of these will require a great deal of small group instruction usually outside the context of the regular classroom. Retention should <u>never</u> be substituted for special education.

Grade Placement

A reasonable rule of thumb suggested by research is that retention presents a valuable programmatic option for kindergarten through second grade. Fourth grade and beyond is usually frowned upon, and third grade is regarded as pivotal. Students retained beyond fourth grade are usually the victims of inappropriate disciplinary action or a lack of special education services or both. Also, self-concept issues seem to take on much greater importance beyond third grade.

Chronological Age

It has been noted in the research that students at highest risk for primary grade failure are males who are also youngest or close to being the youngest in the class. This data should not be considered in isolation but in conjunction with psychosocial and neurological maturity. Another age-related phenomenon has been noted. Parents will occasionally keep a child out of school until the child is one year older in an effort to ensure academic or physical-motor (sports) success or both. This practice is highly questionable, especially for those children who would experience success at their age-appropriate grade.

Previous Retentions

One retention is usually enough. However, with certain handicapped children for whom regular class placement is eventually intended, it may not be completely inappropriate for an age span of two or three years between classmates to exist. Taking into consideration physical, social, emotional, and mental development, some 9- or 10-year old children are well suited for classroom interaction with 6- and 7-year old children.

Nature of the Problem

Two major problems are noted in retention issues: behavior and learning. Retention is almost always considered on the basis of a learning-related difficulty. The gray area arises when a behavior problem contributes to a learning deficit. In that event, determination of first cause may help. Certainly this is very complex and requires in-depth evaluation. Retention should not be considered as a program alternative for a child whose primary problem is behavior unless the behavior is traceable to neurological or psychosocial immaturity or both. Nor should it ever be a substitute for psychotherapeutic intervention for those children whose behavior is traceable to an emotional disorder.

Sex

When it comes to school-related problems, males outnumber females from four to one to nine to one. Implications are that many more males will be considered for retention than females, although what this might mean for decision making is undetermined. The percentage of actual retentions in relation to children suggested for retention may be greater for girls than for boys. Hypothetically, for school personnel to suggest retention for a girl she must be so deficient and the factors so ovewhelmingly in favor of it that merely suggesting it indicates it is a foregone conclusion.

Chronic Absenteeism

Children fall behind in school because of nonattendance. If it can be demonstrated that a child's record of absenteeism is so severe that it becomes an important factor in the child's underachievement, retention might be considered as a way of providing him with the instruction he missed.

Basic Skill Competencies

This factor stands out more than any other because it is the reason most often cited when an educational system wishes to retain a student. For purposes of decision making, competence in grade-level skills may be thought of as adequate, inadequate or severely deficient. Basic skill deficiencies may result from a multitude of factors that interrelate in complex, subtle ways, of which many have already been described. A student who is inadequate or severely deficient in his basic skill acquisition will require an in-depth analysis of the reasons for his difficulties by a multidisciplinary team.

Peer Pressure

The important questions to answer are

1. How susceptible to peer pressure is the student, and what might its impact be on his self-concept?

2. Does the student have very close friends with whom he has formed long-lasting ties, and how will retention affect these relationships?

3. What is the nature of the student's peer relationships outside of school, and with whom does he have these relationships?

4. Does the student live in close proximity to age-mates and classmates, and will retention be a continuing source of embarrassment for him?

Child's Attitude toward Retention

At a time when student input is becoming more and more a part of the educational planning process, it behooves us to turn to the student for the student's own reaction to a possible retention decision. Due to age and maturity factors this often may not be feasible. Although 6-, 7-, and 8- year old children are usually capable of listening and responding to such a discussion, their understanding and ability to judge their own best interests remain questionable. Nevertheless the child's voice should be heard, especially in cases of strenuous personal objections or affirmations.

FAMILY FACTORS

Geographical Moves

It does not appear uncommon for some children to be enrolled in five different schools in six years. The impact on the continuity of the child's education can be staggering. Methods and materials are inconsistent; goals and objectives change; learning, study, and performance patterns are never clearly established. Family transiency may be one of the only factors suggesting retention at grades higher than second or third. It seems easier to retain a student when he is entering a school for the first time. A child entering sixth grade for the second time in a new school system might be given the competitive edge he needs to succeed in junior high school.

Foreign Language Emigrants

This is not necessarily a meaningful factor in and of itself. However, when a language other than English is spoken in the home or the child enters school with a limited exposure to the English language or American culture, this factor may loom larger on the "for retention" side.

Attitude toward Retention

This extremely crucial factor is often a combination of a number of lesser factors:

1. Personal history of retention. One or both parents were retained during their school careers. They have specific, possibly highly emotional thoughts about it in relation to themselves and their children.

2. Cultural attitudes. In certain cultures, open knowledge of school failure in the form of retention is to be shunned at all costs.

3. Pressure from friends, neighbors, and relatives. Because most families are part of a social context comprised of groups of families, this can take on a high measure of significance. Such groups tend to establish rules and norms of their own that tend to be acceptable to even larger social groupings such as neighborhoods, communities, towns, etc. Individual families can be highly susceptible to pressure to conform to these groups. Almost all family groupings strongly value unflawed children who proceed through development and schooling in a normal fashion. Retention implies a flaw that can easily develop into a social stigma in the eyes of the parents of the retained child. Rational problem solving, which presents and weighs clear-cut advan-

tages and disadvantages, is a viable alternative to emotionally charged decision making.

Age of Siblings and Sibling Pressure

This can be a highly significant factor against retention. Younger brothers and sisters who achieve in school can be an ongoing source of irritation and misery for underachieving children. The younger siblings become permanent mirrors, reflecting all that is wrong with the older child's school performance. To be stigmatized by one's peers is no easy burden, but to be stigmatized within one's family may be psychologically overwhelming. The situation that most strongly mitigates against retention may be a highly competitive family in which a younger child is perceived to be performing better in school than an older sibling, and the children are separated by only one grade. Thus if the child were to be retained, he would find himself in the same grade as his younger brother or sister, with potentially devastating results.

Involvement of Family Physician

In many cases of a child's school failure, the family physician is the first professional consulted outside of the school setting. Pediatricians' knowledge of childhood education is extremely variable. Similarly the physician's influence on any particular family varies significantly. However, when this influence does exist and the family physician holds and expresses strong opinions either way, it would be optimal if the education personnel would include the physician in the decision-making process.

SCHOOL FACTORS

School System Attitudes toward Retention

Unfortunately, some systems, by superintendent edict or school board policy statement, declare that retention is not a policy of the school system. Any decision of this nature diminishes the flexibility of the educational system, and decreases in flexibility tend to diminish educational systems. Policy statements regarding retention and other issues are antithetical to the rational decision-making model proposed in this paper. It is hoped that reason will ultimately triumph over doctrine.

Principal's Attitude toward Retention

The building Principal is usually able to set policy within his or her domain. The statements made under "School System Attitudes toward Retention" are applicable here.

Teacher Attitude toward Retention

All school factors previously mentioned apply. Let us assume however that a given teacher is neither for nor against retention but is in conflict over the advantages and disadvantages for an individual student. In such a case, a decision-making model can be of assistance. The classroom teacher who has attempted to teach the child and has not succeeded due to a number of factors may be in the best position to evaluate the potential efficacy of retention. Many times the essential difficulty besides evaluating potential retention is evaluating the nature of the instruction that has been tried and has failed. Usually it is only the individual teacher who can make the assessment of teaching behavior and technique.

Availability of Special Education Services

Retention without some form of special education involvement is meaningless because the child may find himself again in the failing situation that originally led to his retention. Any discussion of retention should always imply a need for services over and above and perhaps different from unmodified, regular classroom programming. The advantages of retention are dealt a serious blow without a provision for special services. It is doubtful that retention in and of itself will work to the benefit of the child.

Availability of Other Programmatic Options

This may be considered a potentially acceptable alternative to retention or special education services or both. Such options might include special language development classes in the primary grades and transition classes. Transition classes that require three years to complete two grades differ from retention primarily in semantics (i.e., a child goes from first grade into a first-second grade combination and then the following year into second grade). The child is essentially being retained. Nevertheless this arrangement is often more acceptable to parents and school personnel because retention tends to lose social stigma if it is presented in the form of a transition class. In settings where a variety of programmatic options exist, retention will be less likely to appear as a primary choice for dealing with the special needs of children.

Availability of Personnel

One rule of thumb might be that the child should never repeat a grade with the same teacher. The reasons are obvious. The child has already failed with this teacher and has established a pattern of teaching-learning interaction with the teacher that has not resulted in successful achievement. The teacher may be frustrated in attempts to teach the child and may have developed negative feelings toward the youngster. The teacher has already tried to modify teaching strategies without beneficial results, and there is no reason to believe that further modifications will result in success.

On the other hand some teachers feel that with some children it takes an inordinate amount of time to assess behavior, habits, learning style, and approaches that will foster maximum performance. These teachers usually feel confident that after one year of working with this child that they can now work together effectively. The answer to this dilemma is found in the amount of trust and

confidence that parents and administrators have in
the particular teacher.

An important consideration in assigning the
child to a new teacher is the possiblity of moving
the child to a different school within the same
system or neighborhood or both. A perceived fresh
start with no attendant history of failure in the
new surroundings could be beneficial to the child.
The newness of the situation would more than
likely outweigh any conflicts resulting from the
retention.

The purpose of this presentation is to promote rational decision making on the part of
school personnel and parents with regard to retention. If it is useful, the ultimate beneficiaries will
be the children.

## G.	Understand the implications of departmentalization at the elementary level.

Departmentalization is a process whereby teachers are assigned to teach certain aspects of the curriculum. Children are then grouped for specific periods of instruction with each teacher. The most obvious result is that elementary age school children must learn to cope with multiple educational settings, teaching styles, instructional strategies, and demands. They are ill-equipped to do so and for many, departmentalization is a barrier to a successful elementary school experience.

There are many more reasons to depict departmentalization, especially in the primary grades, as a potential major contributor to school failure and special education rosters. Departmentalization tends to promote a curriculum focus rather than a child focus. Teachers easily fall into a pattern that upholds the nature of the material to be learned, above the nature of the learner. This emphasis on content promotes a minimal orientation toward the child. This is a considerable error, especially at this point in the child's schooling. Perhaps the single most critical element in education, especially in the primary grades, is the relationship that must be developed between the teacher and the young child. When three and four teachers participate in the daily instruction of young children, the potentially powerful teacher-child relationship may be diminished to a third or fourth of what it should be.

Finally, the curriculum itself is splintered in such a way that students cannot possibly learn to transfer learning. They fail to apply skills learned in one subject to another. The potential for deep insight into the unity and interconnectedness of all things may be completely lost. (For a further discussion on departmentalization at the secondary level, see II. D. 1., page 66.)

H. **Commit to a long term gradual process of moving teachers up and down grades one through six.**

This process is essential for promoting a highly competent teaching staff. One of the most significant gaps in the knowledge, insight, and understanding of teachers is child development and its relation to the curriculum hierarchy. Very few teachers know what children should have learned during each year of schooling and even fewer are able to understand the nature of the child's stages of physical, psycho-social and cognitive growth.

A primary way to turn ignorance into knowledge is to provide the teachers with experience at all grades, one through six, inclusively. This does not mean an administrator should create chaos by moving every teacher every year. It does mean that each year a few teachers should change grades and that there should be a long range plan that provides the opportunity for every teacher to experience every grade, one through six. This might occur across ten or twelve years of teaching. The proposed grade range is by no means meant to be restrictive. However, kindergarten may be too specialized and beyond sixth grade may be too unwieldy or inappropriate.

This proposition was born eight years ago. A fourth grade teacher related that she was able to teach a child in her class who was functioning at a first grade level because she had been a first grade teacher. Her comment was that she knew the first grade curriculum, had easy access to those materials, and could teach to the child's level while working with others on fourth grade material.

Eight years ago this proposition met with unanimous hostility from large and small audiences of regular classroom teachers. Today, it is an idea whose time has come. It is possible that the most powerful, competent elementary school staff ever assembled in one school would be comprised of teachers who have taught at least one year in every grade.

An intermediate step or additional process might be to declare one day each month as "switch day." All elementary staff change to randomly assigned grades and classrooms and pick up where the lesson plan begins for at least part of the day. This can truly be a wonderful learning experience for many teachers who have no idea what younger or older children are like, what their curriculum content is, and what the teaching strategies are.

I. Develop a long range plan for in-service training for teachers and administrators.

In-service training periodically goes through a meat grinder of criticism, and justifiably so. In general, the impact of in-service training is perceived as negligible. Unfortunately, negativity toward it usually generalizes from how it is done to the concept itself. It tends to be a series of one-shot presentations for all concerned with little or no follow-up. The main objective seems to be to find consultants who will not turn school personnel off, rather than find professionals who can provide some meaningful information. Of course, this may be a commentary on available expertise. Many people possess important knowledge and ideas. However, relatively few can get their messages across in palatable form to large and small audiences of classroom teachers and administrators.

There are two positive approaches to this process. The first is that in-service training or staff development requires long term planning. The one-shot strategy should have faded away long ago. In-service Coordinator is not a job to be thrust on some unlucky administrator. The larger school systems have the edge because they might have a full time position designated as In-service Coordinator. Systems that can't afford a separate role must designate the job as part of the continuous role inherent in one position. It should not rotate. Continuity is born out of consistency and consistency has a better chance when one position maintains responsibility.

Five year plans are in order. They should include the long range goals the system wants to attain through staff development. Short term objectives should be specified, along with in-service strategies, potential consultants to meet specific needs, time lines, and a strong evaluation component. As needs shift, modifications might occur over the five year period without necessarily compromising the integrity of the plan as a whole. The original formulation of the plan could be based on a formal needs assessment or some other way in which a general concensus might be reached as to the needs of the system. Some school systems need a benign dictator to set things in motion. Too often, needs assessments can be a camouflage for lack of action and fear of decision-making.

The second staff development consideration is that a certain amount of the in-service budget should be set aside each year to be used to address specific, building level issues that may go far afield from the five year plan. Educational change is primarily thought of as being a top down phenomenon. Handicapped legislation and minimum competency testing are two prime examples. Both have certainly had great impact on the way education is presently conducted. However, education is essentially a human process and the essence of this process is human attitudes. These cannot be legislated. A significant example is bigotry, which is not necessarily driven away by civil rights legislation.

Attitude change is a grass roots phenomenon. It begins with the individual and proceeds upward through the hierarchy of the social system. The way to address attitudes is through generating concrete solutions to everyday problems that teachers and administrators have. The availability of on-going consultation as part of overall in-service is important. Solving an individual child's problem might mean having to change the entire system. An outside consultant can occasionally generate enough catalytic energy to make this happen for everyone's benefit.

J. Educate the community about all legal and regulatory aspects of regular and special education.

Legislation and lawyers can be very frightening for educators. As fear rises, a tendency may develop toward under-informing the public, especially in an in-depth manner. Some educators would prefer to be as close mouthed as possible regarding parent rights and the nature of the school process. The explanation given for this position is that if "they" know too much, "they" will have the knowledge to reinforce a strong adversarial position.

A better educated community is a community that values ecucation, and a community that values education supports the schools. People need to know and have a right to know. People may disagree philosophically, but they only get angry and attack when they think they are being manipulated or kept ignorant.

The fundamental problem of how to educate the community remains. Currently, all methods seem to be lacking. There will always be a nucleus of very interested, enthusiastic parents who attend school functions and join Parent-Teacher Organizations. There remain a whole host of others who are peripheral, depending on whether or not they are personally affected. Open school nights, workshops with national speakers, and report card conferences seldom generate satisfactory numbers. Sometimes five thousand notices are sent out to the community about a weekday evening presentation. Radio and local television spots publicize the event. Local newspapers become part of the media blitz. The evening arrives and the sponsoring school personnel hold their breath because five people may show up or five hundred. No one knows.

Most educators would agree that traditional strategies are not working. Therefore, more radical ones may be required.

1. Hold workshops and presentations for parents on Saturdays or Sundays. Perhaps a light breakfast could be served. Experiment with early evenings, particularly from four to six o'clock (which is just before dinner as opposed to after it).

2. Hold workshops and presentations for parents during the day on weekdays. It means providing baby sitting services at the school for pre-schoolers. A form might be sent home asking parents to choose days of the week that would be most convenient if they had to take off from work for a few hours. Also, attempts should be made to find out what times would be most convenient. Eight o'clock in the morning is worth a try. The audience might be exclusively women, but fathers tend not to come out at any time, which leads to the next point.

3. Try to set up some workshops exclusively for fathers and try to get some commitment from them to attend during the early morning of a work day. There will be some last minute cancellations but that is to be expected.

4. Make periodic school attendance mandatory. Establishing a school system policy that parents must personally pick up their children's report cards can have many positive ramifications. Interacting face to face can immediately change an irrational antagonism into a positive cooperative effort.

5. Promote school based functions such as workshops as a social gathering for parents. Make the parents aware that it can be an important opportunity to meet with their neighbors and become part of a larger social group. Provide wine and cheese and even entertainment after the presentation.

K. Work for greater parent involvement.

The vast majority of parents know mostly everything there is to know about their own children. It is rare
that a child will exhibit a behavioral constellation in school
that the parents are completely unaware of or have never
experienced at home. Yet when it comes to acceptance of
some responsibility for the development, maintenance, or
encouragement of counterproductive behaviors, the parents may balk. This is in spite of these parents genuinely
caring about their children. However, there is a large
difference between caring and truly being involved.

Most children are decent human beings who become
decent adults. It is fairly consistent, perhaps more than
educators are willing to say, that the students who present
the greatest behavioral difficulty to the schools are usually
those students who have uninvolved parents. Often, the
parents don't know what to do themselves. At the times
when the child requires greater supervision (i.e., early
adolescence), he is getting physically bigger and the parents are feeling more and more helpless. The compounding
problem is that many parents expect educators to manage
their children more effectively than they can themselves.
They accept in loco parentis (when the child enters the
schoolhouse door, the school assumes the responsibility of
the parent for that period of time the child is in school),
but won't relinquish the final authority over the child.
Many parents demand that educators control their children
and then prevent educators from carrying out needed consequences.

There are no packaged solutions to this. It is an

ongoing human relations process. Sometimes parents will only get involved when a crisis arises, even after years of suggestion that a crisis will arise unless something is done. There are two major points to consider. The first is that educators and parents do not have a choice between allied and adversarial status. They must be allies. They must do everything in their power as people to become allies and not adversaries. This is an essential aspect of commitment to children. When parents and educators work together everything is possible. When they do not work together, sometimes nothing is possible.

The second point is that educators tend to dismiss parents too easily as being uncooperative or uninvolved or even uncaring. If there isn't an immediate positive response from a parent to some overture made by an educator, the matter may be dropped completely until a crisis occurs. Educators don't try hard enough. Sometimes the only stragegy borders on being a pest. Sooner or later the parent may get the message that school personnel care enough about the child to make pests of themselves. Keeping records of all attempts at communication — phone calls, correspondence, and home visits — promotes awareness of how hard educators are really trying.

II. REGULAR EDUCATION CURRICULUM PROPOSITIONS

A. Generate a heavy emphasis on language development, especially kindergarten through second grade.

It is a virtual certainty that without a competent level of linguistic skill in the form of comprehension and expression of language, the primary grades would be disastrous. Language processing is essentially sequential in nature and so is the major part of academic skill development in American education. There are attempts being made to have teachers develop language teaching strategies that are wholistic rather than sequential. To date, these inroads are far too few to create a major change. After all, the teachers themselves have been successfully educated by a system that adheres to a linguistically based, sequential approach.

Given this reality, the suggestion is not that wholistic approaches be abandoned. Rather, they should continue to be pursued as viable, while simultaneously raising the level of teaching competence for sequential tasks. A good example of knowledge that is only now beginning to permeate instruction is that the basic skills of reading, writing and spelling have a great deal to do with linguistic competence. What is finally being understood is that children who do poorly in these areas, especially reading, and particularly in the early primary grades, are usually not competent in underlying linguistic skill such as vocabulary and syntax. Visual perceptual problems and motor coordination deficits may be highly correlated with reading problems. However, language deficits may be considered directly causative. Reading is language. How can one expect a child to learn to read when his language skills are undeveloped or deficient?

School systems should be committed to a heavy emphasis on language development, especially kindergarten through second grade. This emphasis should be expressed through primary teachers' curriculum guides and the establishment of a self-contained regular class, almost exclusively devoted to language development. Kindergarten screening will usually determine those children who might be eligible for such a class. The class size should not exceed sixteen, unless there is an aide. Children whould have the option of attending this language development class from kindergarten through second grade. Learning to read should be de-emphasized, while books, stories, and words become the heart of class activity. It should be explained to the parents at the outset that many of these children might not be ready to start formally learning to read until third grade or approximately age eight. Until that time, the children will be given all the linguistic prerequisites in order to insure success.

The results could be profound, particularly in relation to the intent of this guide. Instead of having sixteen children who are functioning at first grade level upon entry into third grade, there could be sixteen normal children who are ready to begin reading in third grade. Instead of having sixteen special education referrals on children who have failed for three years and are discrepant enough to warrant someone calling them handicapped or dyslexic, there are sixteen children who succeeded in a regular education program geared to their needs and are now ready for the next step.

B. Revamp the curriculum in accordance with the acknowledged existence of slow learners.

This is another point with potential major impact. Many educators don't know what slow learner means because the third word in the phrase is not used. It is slow learning <u>rate</u>. Educators should be the last to impose arbitrary limits on what children can learn. We must assume that all children can and do learn, but sometimes the curriculum marches and the children crawl. The gap widens. They need more time and more practice, and perhaps, more emphasis on activity and concrete doing than abstract, symbolic manipulation.

There as many eighty and eighty-five I.Q. children as there are one hundred and fifteen and one hundred and twenty I.Q. chldren. Public education owes the former group as much as the latter. All students deserve the best possible program suited to their needs and geared to helping them develop to their fullest potential. Examining the history of mainstreaming, it becomes evident that the slow learning rate child was the original student for whom mainstreaming was intended. Regular education has generally failed in its attempts (if there have been any) to effectively program for these children. The vast majority are receiving special education services that border on trying to put bandaids on hemophiliacs. The rest of their time is spent struggling under regular classroom conditions and curriculum standards that are far removed from consideration for their slow learning rate.

The following options for these students have been delineated in one form or another by various authors:

1. Retain the same objectives as the regular class curriculum, but allow the students to move more slowly, one small step at a time.

2. Establish and adopt a parellel curriculum utilizing the same core subjects.

3. Utilize the same regular education curriculum, but lower the expectations for work output by some factor.

4. Eliminate parts of the regular education curriculum by establishing priorities and making value judgments in cooperation with students and parents.

5. Drop non-essential subtasks of the regular education curriculum.

There are exceptions, but most of the slow learning rate students should be removed from the roles of special education and fully normalized. This requires a system accommodation. The child is who he is. It is the system that must respond.

Recently, a number of State Departments of Education have eliminated the category of "slow learner" from their regulations under their state special education laws. This is right and wrong. Conceptually, it is the correct response. It confirms the message that these children are the responsibility of regular education. However, if the regular education system is not ready to accommodate these students either attitudinally or with specific resources, it is wrong. The children will be doomed to failure. Everyone will benefit from a commitment to provide an appropriate education for the slow learning rate student.

C. **Establish appropriate school behavior as a curriculum unto itself.**

All too often, regular educators view inappropriate school behavior as an obstacle or barrier to the "real" purpose of education, which is supposedly academic learning. This promotes a feeling of guilt on the part of any teacher who must use academic time to deliver discipline or use behavior management strategies. Unfortunately, that feeling of guilt can be a major obstacle to effective discipline and behavior management.

At the present time, it is not uncommon to find every child who calls out without raising his hand being sent for a full IEP evaluation. This is partially a commentary on the apparent lack of effective teaching of appropriate school behavior, which is linked directly to how this teaching is conceptualized. The recommendation is that appropriate school behavior become as much a part of the curriculum as academics. The major difference is that academic subjects are usually laid out in blocks of time, whereas behavior occurs throughout the school day in every context. For this reason, there must be schoolwide behavior policies and an evaluation of teachers that is partially based on the consistency of their attempts to enforce behavioral standards.

Ineffective discipline is usually the result of a splintered system (i.e., departmentalization). The inherent inconsistency of many adults reacting differently to many situations, promotes an inherent behavioral inconsistancy. The commitment to appropriate school behavior requires an approach that dictates responsibility and the acceptance of school behavior as equal in importance to academic learning.

Educators usually try to accomplish this through in-service workshops dealing with effective discipline and behavior management. However, this can become another example of generating potentially good information and strategies without having the mechanism to make them happen. Ideas are only as good as their capability for implementation. A general orientation toward creating a school behavior curriculum is a key. This might be accomplished through staff meetings, with the agenda being staff input on drawing up a school and classroom behavior curriculum, complete with goals, objectives, strategies, and evaluation criteria.

An example of a specific strategy geared to committing the staff to this process is to establish a time-out room. Most teachers would agree that classroom disruption should not be tolerated and that it is indefensible to sacrifice twenty-five students in a clasroom to periodic disruptive behavior on the part of one or two. Sending these students to the Principal's office seldom solves the problem and can promote an even greater desire to be removed from class. A time-out room is required. It may be conceptualized in many different ways. For example, crisis intervention and counseling, punishment in the form of restriction to seat, silence, and no activity, or having to do schoolwork in order to earn one's return to the classroom. Special educators have used many different forms of time-out as an effective behavior management strategy for many years. Yet regular educators do not seem to have the space for a time-out room, nor a staff person to supervise such a room.

Committing the staff to such a process would require locating a proper space and dividing up blocks of time in order to provide continuous supervision of the room. Also, there would have to be a consensus as to the approach used. Another possiblity is to enlist the aid of those teachers who are able to deal effectively with many rule breaking students through sheer force of will. They may be willing to be the designated receivers of students who have to be removed from class. It seems to be even more effective when the receiving teachers are in grades well above or below the grade of the removed student. This type of strategy does more than attempt to help the student succeed in his regular classroom. It unites the staff. It enables them to actively engage in a schoolwide behavior curriculum and to know that they will be supported in this critical endeavor.

One more example is worth mentioning. It was published as "The Homework Solution" in the Aug./Sept., 1983 Journal of Learning Disabilities and is reproduced in this guide. It is another way to demonstrate that school behavior can be taught, and should be taught, on an equal footing with academics.

THE HOMEWORK SOLUTION

Laurence M. Lieberman, EdD
Associate Editor

For ten years, I have been working on the problem of students not doing homework. I had never solved the problem satisfactorily for myself or for the students — until yesterday. (It may have been the day before yesterday.)

I was talking to two sixth-grade teachers and admiring the same situation that had existed for seven months. One of their students does his homework — sometimes. The teachers never seem to know when or in what condition it will be passed in. Furthermore, the most demonstrative behavior elicited by the teacher from the student for incomplete and/or inappropriate homework assignments has been a shrug, with or without palms turned upward. This scene is repeated so often and in so many schools across America that it almost has become folklore, like American Gothic. What ensues are excuses, lies, bad grades, incompletes, after-school detentions, negative or positive parent involvement, and incredible hassles with teachers.

These are the givens:

1. Homework creates significant problems between teachers and students. All else may be excellent, but lack of well-done homework assignments can crush a potentially excellent teacher-student relationship. Most teachers take lack of homework as a direct affront to their authority.

2. Teachers cannot directly control homework. By definition, it is to be done outside of

their purview. Therefore, it is a test of a teacher's authority that goes even beyond the limits of the school building. It is a contest that teachers, despite being armed with the ability to give bad grades (akin to rocks against tanks), cannot possibly win.

3. When it comes to homework, parents are easily duped by their own children. Time is an issue. Effort and energy are issues. Many times the parents can't do the homework themselves. Also, standing over your own child in attempt to have him complete his homework is not the path to enlightened parent-child relationships. Making sure to sign the homework every evening sometimes works but the consistency usually falls apart.

4. When parents are brought into the situation, their own effectiveness as parents comes under the direct scrutiny of teachers. Many times the student still does not do his homework; only now, the parents are implicated as well! And they find themselves in a hassle with the teachers.

5. The usual strategy for lack of homework or unacceptable homework is an after-school detention, where the student is asked to complete the assignments he has not done.

The vast majority of students will verbalize the fact that they hate to stay after school to do their homework. Yet, the consequence of detention does little or nothing to alter the behavior of erratic homework producers.

In view of all these emotionally laden statements, the solution seems relatively simplistic and therein lies its power. All we must do is reconceptualize homework, thereby completely reversing the process. Students must earn the privilege of being allowed to do homework at home. Everyone begins with the premise that homework is to be done at home. However, a student who fails to comply has demonstrated an inability to do so and is therfore placed on a five day probation. He must stay after school for five consecutive days and report to the "homework room" to do his homework within an agreed upon period of time. Follow-up consists of doing homework at home and school every other day for five days, and then full-time homework at home. One slip-up results in another five day in-school probationary period.

The meaningfulness of this approach can be profound. First, there is no longer a choice to do homework or not to do homework. The only choice is to do it in school or to do it at home. Second, the positive consequence is the ability to do homework at home, as opposed to the negative consequence of the student staying after school for not completing the homework. The process is reversed. To paraphrase the actor in the stockbroker commercial, "Kids get to do homework the old-fashioned way. They earn it."

What does it take to implement this plan? It takes the same ingredients as any strategy that hasn't worked in the past with one major exception: it's easier. The only parent cooperation required is that they allow the child to remain after school. Most school systems have a "late bus" to provide transportation or if need be have the parents pick up the students. It requires teachers who are willing to stay after school and put forth the effort to get the job done. There are always teachers of this caliber available. Usually the system doesn't use them to their best potential. The key is follow-up, follow-up and more follow-up. The students will test the system. The system will deliver.

I'll put myself on the line on this one. I dare anyone to write to me and tell me it doesn't work. If you do write, you'd better send me another solution.

D. Examine specific strategies for secondary school programs.

If the premises on which this guide is based are accepted, then the following conclusion is evident. Barring physical or emotional trauma, no student should be referred to special education for the first time in the junior or senior high school. If he is, and he is determined to be genuinely handicapped, educators failed the child earlier in his life and it must be investigated. The system itself is failing if handicaps begin in junior or senior high school.

Many of the propositions cut across all grades and school circumstances. However, there are additional considerations for the secondary school. The regular education–special education interface at this level requires some special examination.

1. Departmentalization

This has already been addressed as a potential barrier to a successful elementary school experience. The same holds true at the secondary level. The junior high school has been a particular target of this claim for many years. Twelve and thirteen year olds can be extremely disorganized, irresponsible, and easily overwhelmed. They do not necessarily generate their own glue in trying to piece together a piece-meal educational process. They are sent to five different teachers, who are teaching five different subject matter areas in five different ways. The educational system is pulling students apart, and no one is putting them back together. If they fail, they usually end up being referred to special education.

The obvious and potentially very successful solution to this problem is to establish one or more self-contained regular education classrooms at the junior-senior high school level. Science and Math, and English and Social Studies, can be taught by two teachers. The teachers change classes while the students stay together within their own classrooms. Consistent grading, and performance and behavioral standards can be addressed much more easily. These students should be red flagged by teachers at the end of the year (the year preceding entry to junior high and/or senior high), as students who are high risk for a departmentalized curriculum. Predictably, these are the students who would be referred for a special education evaluation by November of any given year. These same students would probably be discipline problems for a great many teachers. Maintaining them in one classroom for major subjects could prevent all these potential problems and give them a chance to succeed.

This is another approach at the cutting edge. It is another regular education program alternative that is not generally tried prior to calling for special education intervention. In the case of over-dependence on departmentalization practices, the system is not only not trying to solve regular education-special education problems, it is contributing to them.

2. Study skills and test taking.

There are many students who fail in regular education because they don't know how to study and take tests. This is true for normal students as well as those with learning and behavior problems. A significant comment from secondary subject matter teachers is that the special education students can often participate in class, do the work, and learn. They just can't pass the tests. Consequently they fail, and their efforts go for naught in terms of grades and credits.

The first week of every school year, starting in seventh grade and proceeding through senior in high school, should be devoted to a course for all students in study skills and test taking. Almost every major educational publisher has quality materials on this topic in the form of curriculum guides and suggested activities leading to greater competence. The course should be taught as a refresher each year by the subject teachers. In that way, they can modify the material and introduce their own expectations. Also, differences will emerge as to how to study Social Studies as opposed to Math, which may require a different orientation entirely.

Another significant strategy is to develop triple level testing. Some subjects, if not all, lend themselves to be easily organized into units with unit tests. These tests can be standardized across teachers of that subject. In addition, they can be presented in the following manner.

Level three tests are the most concrete and require the least amount of student output (i.e., true-false, multiple choice). Level two might require more abstract thought and involve matching, fill-ins, and some short written explanations. Level one would be the most abstract and require the most explanation. Parents, teacher and student could meet to determine which level test would be appropriate for that particular student. The highest mark associated with level three would be C+, level two a B+, and level one, an A. If the student achieved in the top twenty-five percent on any given level test, he could choose to take the next higher level test in an attempt to better his grade. The teacher would eliminate the lower of his two marks.

One more popular strategy is worth mentioning. Many students suffer from anxiety and pressure resulting from timed tests. Certainly arrangements could be made for some students to have a reasonably extended period of time when taking exams.

3. Counseling.

The adolescent needs a great deal of adult caring, support, and continuous involvement through the vicissitudes of this period. The system must find ways to exhume the guidance counselors and school psychologists from their paper tombs and promote greater interaction with students. It may require a survey of how time is spent and a reorganization of that time, that will impact more directly on the students.

For example, a recent survey of twenty school psychologists working for a large Special Education Cooperative revealed that there is no standardized test battery common to all. Furthermore, the same referral might result in one hour's worth of testing or four hour's worth of testing, depending on who was doing the testing. Perhaps what is needed is a standardized minimum battery that could be followed up in greater depth if deemed necessary. For the most part, the psychologists seemed to use the same tests anyway. It was only a question of how many they used. In this manner, time could be conserved and utilized for other important purposes. There must be more than lip service given to the desire to do more counseling. Too often, the same people who bemoan their lack of time to do meaningful things, end up buried under paper when the opportunity for meaningful interaction presents itself.

4.   Cluster teams.

Another consideration might be called a "cluster team approach." The students are grouped in classes and then travel from teacher to teacher as a class. This promotes group cohesion, better discipline, and a much greater knowledge of the students across subject matter teachers.   A block of time might be set aside each week for planning and teacher coordination.   The teachers would have an opportunity to meet and discuss the students and work out solutions to perceived problems because they would all have the same students. This approach also helps to break down the barriers erected by each department within a departmentalized system.

5.   Homogeneous grouping.

Arguments continuously abound regarding homogeneous versus heterogenous grouping. For many, homogeneous grouping or tracking are dirty words. In fact, tracking is illegal if done solely on the basis of standardized achievement test scores. In Hobson v. Hansen (1967), the U.S. Supreme Court ruled that tracking (ability grouping) based on standardized tests that are not relevant to many minority students, violates both the due process and equal protection guarantees of the Fourteenth Amendment.   It can be a highly charged issue. There are many reasons to believe that heterogeneity in classrooms has a much greater chance for success at the elementary level, and indeed, should be pursued to the greatest extent possible. However, junior-senior high school may be another matter entirely.

The argument that the students are depicted by the system as being low enders doesn't seem to hold up. If the students are low enders, they know who they are and so does everyone else. In fact, they may be low enders because they are wiped out by the level of instruction and demands made in wide ranging heterogeneous groups. They may need to be grouped for instructional purposes in such a way that the curriculum might be tailored to their needs. Secondary educators generally consider grouping only for English and Mathematics. This is an error. Besides English, Social Studies may be the most desirable target for this strategy. It would be rare to find ninth grade Social Studies being taught effectively to students ranging in I.Q. from seventy-five to one hundred and thirty-five and having third to twelfth grade level reading skills. Grouping for instructional purposes may be a necessary evil.

A general problem related to tracking is a type of "spread phenomenon." The student is either placed in a high track for all subjects or a low track for all subjects, regardless of aptitude or achievement in a particular subject. When tracking students for instructional purposes, educators should make every effort to maintain a considerable level of flexibility.

Another primary problem resulting from instructional grouping is that students with behavior problems tend to be grouped with slow learners. There is no satisfactory solution short of setting up two homogeneous groups. Recognition and close monitoring of potential problems is critical.

6.   Academic support and skill development

At the junior-senior high school level, special education resource teachers become trapped into being subject matter tutors, instead of continuing to pursue skill development with their students. The pressure on the student is to get the report written, not on learning how to write it. However, having it done is not the same as having done it. The students need both. They continue to need help in developing their skills while they may also need help in getting through the course material. Usually one or the other is not available and the special education teachers and the students succumb to the pressure of regular education, moving away from skills and toward content. This can result in high school graduates who are virtually illiterate.

Some districts have instituted extra help sessions for the students after school, so as to enable a greater focus on skills in special education resource rooms. Most often, this is not available due to union contracts and other restrictions on teacher time. An old model has been largely neglected in recent years: home tutoring. With the rise of resource room programming, it seems that the home tutoring model has greately declined. Adolescents who are free from the pressures of appearing "dumb" in the resource room may benefit from some intensive one on one work in the privacy of their own homes. The suggestion is not necessarily that the school system pay for this, although some might. Many parents can afford a certain amount per hourly rate for a teacher or college student, or even a mature, competent high school student to provide specific subject tutoring.

7. Discipline policy and parent involvement.

A consistent and well articulated discipline policy is mandatory. The students need it, want it, and it is in everyone's best interests to see to it that it is enforced. Every effort should be made to include the parents in the process. The following is an illustration. Budget cuts result in program and service cuts. Occasionally, the cutting knife is used on the late bus, which has traditionally been the way to implement after–school–detention as a disciplinary policy. When the late bus disappears, so does the possibility of detention. A form letter could be drafted and sent home that might read: "If we want to keep your child after school until five o'clock in the afternoon for disciplinary reasons, will you or will you not come to the school and pick him up, and if not, why not?"

Most parents would commit themselves to such a process. They would seldom arrive at the school at five o'clock in a frame of mind that would question the school's efforts on behalf of their child.

8. Monitoring

Finally, close monitoring is required. With monitoring in place, prevention moves from words to action. Adolescents, especially those with problems beyond the normal ones, are usually somewhat disorganized, ovewhelmed and irresponsible. Educators wait until the students encounter great difficulty and failure, test them, and then declare them disorganized, overwhelmed, and irresponsible. Monitoring requires the involvement of many different school personnel, who would meet with a few students (who need it) at the end of each day to determine if they:

(a) understand the current classwork
(b) understand the current homework assignment
(c) have a plan for studying and doing assignments

If negative results are predictable from these daily interactions, some type of action may be warranted.

An example of a schoolwide program of monitoring (and quite a bit more) is a high school family plan. Each teacher whose seniors have graduated, is assigned an equal number (perhaps 15 or 20) of incoming freshmen and spends the next four years as combination den mother, houseparent, and confidant to this same group. Weekly meetings are held to resolve school problems, and participate in group discussion that may occasionally border on group therapy.

III. SPECIAL EDUCATION PROGRAM PROPOSITIONS

A. Prioritize severely handicapped in accordance with P.L. 94-142 and most state laws.

It is fairly clear, both in language and intent, that legislation for the handicapped is primarily for those individuals who fall on the severe end of the spectrum. It is also apparent that legislative mandates were established for the handicapped, not for special education. The implication is that one cannot legislate how the educational needs of the severely handicapped are to be met, just that they should be met. This allows for wide variation in programming efforts and even promotes creativity, particularly in the realm of low incidence handicaps and the delivery of services in rural areas.

It is obvious in many school systems, that least restrictive enviromnent thinking has resulted in the opposite priorty; the mildly handicapped. There is some validity to the reasoning that unless the mildly handicapped are served effectively, they will become moderately and severely handicapped. If small deficiencies and discrepancies are not attended to, they can become large deficiencies and discrepancies. Yet evidence for this is flimsy, unless handicaps are defined solely in terms of school performance. For example, experience demonstrates that children who have not successfully integrated basic skills by the end of third grade will probably be even further behind by the end of sixth grade. This assumes that the level of intensity of the special education services is not substantially increased, which it seldom is.

Generally, children who have not acquired third grade skills by the end of third grade, tend to be globally immature or lagging in development in many areas: social, emotional, cognitive, and physical. Their rate of development may be entirely normal for them. Yet they are perceived as lagging in development by people who have very narrow perspectives on how children should perform at certain times in their lives. Intensive special education services delivered during the first three grades may not necessarily prove to be beneficial. Immature children tend to be more active, have shorter attention spans, are more distractible and impulsive, and are just not "ready" to handle the kinds of tasks associated with basic skill acquisition. Waiting beyond sixth grade for maturation to occur seems excessive. Furthermore, adolescent attitudes and motivation can play a major role in whether or not the student will benefit from special education instruction. This seems to narrow the critical time frame for intensive instruction to grades four through six. Any child who has not successfully acquired basic skills by the end of third grade should be a candidate for some form of more intensive instruction. The student may not be able to learn effectively in a large group setting and may require an alternative. However, unless that child is designated as being handicapped, by criteria that is not solely school performance criteria, special education should not necessarily be the alternative.

Another reason given for prioritizing mildly handicapped programming is an ethical-moral choice. Some educators believe that resources should be used primarily on behalf of those children who can reap the most benefit. The problem with this postion is obvious. It places a priori limitations on children who are thought to be more severely handicapped. Educators who would prioritize services to the severely handicapped might argue that a civilized society, by definition, owes the most it can give to those who are not "created equal." There would be no winner in a discussion of the ethics of both positions, which is why the legislation and its intent should be upheld.

The major reasons for an emphasis on children with mild problems are tied to non-categorical programing, mainstreaming, generic teacher training, and a resultant quick-fix mentality. The historical goal of special education was to provide a comprehensive education to the handicapped child that would give him success, and an opportunity to participate to the fullest extent possible in "life, liberty, and the pursuit of happiness." The current goal of special education is to get the child back into regular education. The special educators who espouse this as a higher value, do so on the basis of societal integration and a perception that regular education is "normal," and the vehicle through which the previously stated lofty goals may be attained. While the rationale may be noble, too much may be sacrificed, especially on an individual basis. With the goal being regular class placement, special education will only be as good as regular education allows it to be. Sometimes, regular education is far less than what special education used to be.

Prioritizing the severely handicapped will help everyone to understand the nature of special education. It will help to straighten out the confusion of the regular education–special education interface, and enable people to more effectively define their roles as to who is doing what to whom, where, when, why, and how.

B. Tighten eligibility criteria for special education services and the definition of a handicapped child.

A major aspect of this complex problem is that one part of this two part process is often neglected. In order to receive special education, a child must be declared handicapped <u>and</u> be considered to be in need of special services. It is usually the former condition that is forgotten and the result is a tautology. The definition of a special education child (no longer a handicapped child) is a child in need of special education. One does not need experts to advise as to whether or not a child needs help. Most of the evaluations conducted in schools are for determining the need for help, rather than the existence of a genuine handicap. Of course the determination of a handicap can be extremely complicated and requires multidisciplinary input. Physical disabilities are much more obvious than emotional disturbance, learning disabilities, and mild mental retardation. The impulse might be to think of physical disability and handicap as virtually synonymous, while always maintaining a wait and see attitude toward "hidden handicaps."

This is the realm of professional competence and decision-making. All manner of cut-off scores are to be avoided whenever possible. Sometimes they are the only option because professional expertise is lacking. In the main, cut-off scores have no place when it comes to decisions regarding children's lives. People who don't know how to paint use paintings with numbers on them. People who know how to paint do not need numbers. Different viewpoints and perspectives are needed to arrive at a conclusion. No one is right. No one is wrong. No one owns the truth. Everyone owns a piece of the truth. Competence in this realm is the ability to put the pieces together so that they form a meaningful whole in terms of the child, the nature of his needs, and how best to meet them.

The road to determining the existence of a handicap is the road back. Some people today are calling for the articulation of a new philosophy of special education and the nature of handicapping conditions. What is needed is the old philosophy, back to a time when a handicap was not defined solely on the basis of school performance. When a true handicap exists it is most often a multiple handicap. It can pervade every aspect of a person's cultural, physical, and psychological life. School functioning is only one aspect and must be placed in proper perspective. The consequences of not doing this are familiar. The handicapped student makes it through school with or without special education services and goes on to a long life of continuing to be handicapped, with a possibly diminished quality of living. The school may have been able to enhance his life in school, but what about his life? What is really required for the handicapped is an ILP (Individualized Life Plan), not an IEP.

If one accepts the premise that being successful in school does not necessarily lead to success in life, especially for the handicapped, then one can conclude that success in school, at least in its present form, may not be all that important for some children. For these reasons, school cannot and should not be the primary focus for an evaluation of the existence of a handicap. Handicapped children tend to not do well in regular education formats because they are handicapped. They are not handicapped because they perform poorly in school. The clarity of this point is most evident in examining P.L. 94-142. It is obvious that the law was intended for handicapped children whose school needs were not being met. It was not the intention to determine handicap based on a perceived need for something other than standard regular education practices.

The second step in the process is usually less complex. Once it is determined that the child is handicapped, the nature of his handicap must be linked to his school performance. When this occurs, the process as a whole has been regained. Special education can resume its commitment to the handicapped. It can resume its integrity without compromising regular education. Regular education responsibility can be upheld for those aspects of schooling where compensation can be upheld.

No handicapped child has ever been "fixed" in special education and sent back to the regular class. This message must be used with those who have the singular referral agenda of "take him out of my room." No matter how much the handicapped child is removed, when he returns, he will be a handicapped child. Sometimes the handicapped child may no longer be in need of special education, but this is relatively uncommon. This leads to a significant issue plaguing special educators. It seems that once a child is designated as being in need of special education, he is forever consigned to this designation and these services. Many professionals argue against this as unnecessary and possibly detrimental to the child. This side of the argument is usually based solely on a skills definition of education. It seeks to portray school as a series of skills to be mastered. Presumably, once this occurs, the handicapped child is "fixed" and therefore not handicapped any longer, at least in relation to that skill.

This tends to be an overly simplistic approach to the nature of handicapping conditions. Where they truly exist, even mildly handicapped children may always require some specialized support. After all, the skills disrupted by a handicap are potentially endless. This is not to say that the level or intensity of services should not change over time. The vast majority of children who do get permanently "fixed," probably weren't handicapped to begin with.

C. Return to traditional ways of thinking about the learning disabled child.

Learning disabilities is a special case. Some consider it singularly responsible for the difficulties associated with the special education–regular education interface. As the dictionary definition of a learning disability has gained in popularity, the situation has become worse. The dictionary definition says that if a child isn't learning commensurate with his peers and/or his perceived ability, then he must have a disability; a learning disability.

Professionals who subscribe to this view have no understanding of history and background and the conceptual evolution of the field. The idea of presumed central nervous system impairment being at the core of the problem has never been abandoned by the most prominent experts. Even the newest definition, agreed upon by every major organization involved in the field of learning disabilities, with the exception of ACLD, makes reference to, "these disorders are intrinsic to the individual and presumed to be due to central nervous system dysfunction." For the time being, ACLD is maintaining the 1969, P.L. 91-230, Title VI, Part G definition which similarly states, "such disorders include such conditions as perceptual handicaps, brain injury, minimal brain dysfunction, dyslexia, and developmental aphasia."

A return to traditional ways of thinking means the recognition of learning disabilities as a syndrome, a constellation of symptoms that goes far beyond basic skills. Basic skill deficiencies are considered to be symptoms of underlying neurological disorders. Learning disabilities is a life handicap, not just a school based or academic skill handicap. There are great differences within the learning disabilities population. There is also a continuum of mild, moderate, and severe disorders. Furthermore, it should be understood that the vast majority of children called learning disabled in the schools today are created. They are not born. They are a function of school-child interaction effects and therefore are not true examples of handicapped children. There may be two distinct groups contained within the field, both having one significant commonality; they achieve poorly in school. One group of children are truly disabled. The other group of children are LD, but learning different, not disabled.

One of the greatest errors of judgment in recent years is found in P.L. 94-142 and its approach to learning disabilities. It says that one or more of the following characteristics are associated with being learning disabled: a severe discrepancy between achievement and intellectual ability in oral expression, listening comprehension, written expression, basic reading skill, reading comprehension, mathematics calculation, mathematics reasoning, and spelling.

Who among us is not deficient in at least one of these areas? If it isn't one, then how many of these deficits does one need in order to be learning disabled? This is an unfortunate but valid question; unfortunate because it has no answer. There are no cut-offs. There is only competent, multidisciplinary decision-making. Depending on age and a multitude of complex interacting factors, a child with one of the above discrepancies may be significantly handicapped, while another child with two or three will remain relatively unimpaired.

D. Provide an analysis to the regular education staff that addresses the potential problems inherent in non-categorical special education practices.

Few regular classroom teachers would think that the highly significant special education issue of non-categorical programming could have direct consequences for them. Non-categorical special education is the result of a movement begun in the 1960's to de-label and hopefully to de-stigmatize the handicapped. Although there are only two states that have legislated a generic term (i.e., special needs) as opposed to traditional categories, a recent National Association for Children and Adults with Learning Disabilities survey* found that the vast majority of local school systems throughout the United States have some non or cross or multicategorical programming. These are mostly in the form of generic resource rooms. This is in spite of state legislation maintaining separate categories and by implication, mandates for separate programs. Furthermore, Public Law 94-142 maintains a traditional categorical approach.

While non-categorical programming may solve some administrative problems and even some children's problems at the milder end of the handicapped spectrum, it may

---

* Final Report, Committee on Cross-Categorical Resource Programs of the Association for Children and Adults with Learning Disabilities, Inc. March, 1982.

create a host of other problems that speak directly to regular education responsibility. When traditional labels are dropped, differential diagnosis is replaced by a focus on school performance, to the exclusion of all other considerations. In other words, the new definition of a handicap is poor school performance or school becomes a new handicapping condition. Some states even have a category called "Educationally Handicapped." If the child does not have to be declared impaired, defective, disturbed, disabled, exceptional, or handicapped in order to receive special education services, then all he needs to be is different or discrepant with regard to where his classroom teacher thinks he should be in terms of learning or performance or behavior. It is easy to understand how this could lead to over-referral and under-responsibility.

School based problem children may be skimmed off the top for special education services, while the truly mildly handicapped may be underserved. The distinction to be made is that a mild handicapping condition would be chronic, and might always require some form of special consideration, while school based problems should be remediated and services terminated in the shortest possible time.

Non-categorical practices have infiltrated special education teacher training programs. Arguments abound regarding their efficacy, yet many special education administrators would be hard pressed to select teachers who were competent with the full or even partial range of different handicapped children. In order to teach handicapped children effectively, in-depth knowledge of the nature of that handicapping condition is required. Teachers who graduate from these university based programs are certified in all handicaps. They seem to know a little bit about a lot of things, but surface knowledge does not promote successful teaching. The cycle will swing back toward specialization because the void left by generic-behavioral thinking is becoming more and more evident. Furthermore, with non-categorical programming, learning disabled, emotionally disturbed, and mentally retarded children are placed together for instructional purposes, which might be inappropriate for all involved.

Non-categorical special education contributes to the perspective that special education is the panacea for all of regular education's problems. This raises the significant question of the purpose of special education and whether or not it should be reserved for handicapped children or used to fix regular education problems. It cannot do both, and it certainly cannot be the solution for regular education's difficulties. The primary choice must be for services to the handicapped. When special education steps or is pushed over the line to meet the needs of children with school based problems, its own empire building continues and is strengthened. While special education engages in empire building, regular classroom teachers lose jobs. The result is larger class sizes and consequently, more children with problems. Special education ends up building bigger empires. This is counterproductive for the system as a whole and the students in general, although it appears that at least special education benefits from these circumstances. However, trying to be all things to all people is precarious at best and almost always leads to failure.

E. Have resource room teachers move toward consultation and teaching groups of handicapped children in regular classrooms.

Most special education teachers are not trained as consultants. Most states do not have teacher certification for special education consultants, nor do the local education agencies have jobs for people designated as special education consultants. This is a chicken-egg problem. Certification, legislation, and training create jobs; the need for a particular job creates certification, legislation, and training. Where a consultant position does exist, there may be one or two for an entire school sytem, and it is conceptualized as a full time position. It doesn't have to be. Resource room teachers could schedule children into their rooms four days a week. On the fifth day, they could circulate in regular classrooms, providing the support for regular classroom teachers that is so often lacking. Special education gives much lip service to prevention, yet it is locked into a discrepancy model. First the child must fail. Then something will be done about it. This process may be prevented through special education personnel providing consultation in regular classrooms. There is tremendous potential for on-site modification that can take place prior to a formal pre-referral, referral and diagnostic procedure. Furthermore, once a child is deemed eligible for special education, continued placement in a regular class setting would require ongoing consultation and support.

In all forms of consultation, the onus should be on the consultant to provide a match of strategies, materials, and teaching style with the nature of the classroom teacher and how he or she provides instruction. There are two general questions that must be addressed by would-be consultants. What does one consult with and how does one consult? The first question encompasses the following:

A. Skills and competencies
   1. knowledge of formal and informal assessment
   2. teaching strategies, methods, and techniques
   3. knowledge of materials
   4. behavior management strategies
   5. observational skills
   6. planning and writing objectives
   7. organizational skills

B. An educational philosophy that coincides with or complements that of the community, school, and/or classroom teacher. For example:
   1. citizenship
   2. basic skills
   3. thinking and problem solving
   4. career and vocation
   5. higher education
   6. emotional and social maturity and responsibility
   7. self-actualization
   8. education as a process
   9. least restrictive environment
  10. normalization

           11.   whole child considerations

C.   Knowledge of regular education.

           1.   materials

           2.   methods

           3.   grade level curriculum goals

D.   Knowledge of handicapped children

           1.   literature

           2.   research

           3.   specialized needs

E.   Knowledge of the classroom teacher.

           1.   classroom environment

           2.   space

           3.   levels of difficulty

           4.   methods

           5.   testing

           6.   materials

           7.   pace

           8.   goals and expectations

           9.   motivation and enthusiasm

          10.   organization

          11.   planning

          12.   consistency

How consultation is accomplished involves the following:

A.   Physical characteristics

           1.   gender

           2.   perceived age

           3.   ethnic background

           4.   appearance

B. Personality characteristics
  1. outgoing
  2. can discuss issues instead of people
  3. can see the perspective of the other
  4. effective listener
  5. effective communicator
  6. open and honest
  7. willing to take risks
  8. willing to take responsibility
  9. orientation toward action
C. Professional credibility.
D. Ability to use tact and tactics.
  1. manipulation
  2. support
  3. guilt
  4. flattery
  5. praise
E. Understanding the art of negotiation.
  1. arbitration
  2. mediation
  3. compromise
F. Reality base.
  1. implementable ideas
  2. knowledge of constraints
G. Child advocacy.

Consultation can be extended far beyond a single child emphasis. One such approach borders on regular education/special education team teaching in regular classrooms. Special education teachers would spend the majority of their day in regular classrooms working with the teachers and all the children. No distinction would be made concerning which teacher works with which children or which children are considered to be handicapped and part of special education. This type of approach can certainly go a long way toward promoting educational responsibility for all children.

F. Understand the significance of minimum competency testing and provide alternatives for handicapped students receiving some form of special education.

There are numerous issues attached to minimum competency testing for the handicapped. They are far different from those of standardized achievement testing. These issues can be fairly easily resolved if choices are made based on genuine evaluation of the student's capabilities.

The primary prerequisite for addressing choices and building flexibility is something that was covered earlier; the fundamental decision that in order to be receiving special education services, a child must be designated as being handicapped and in need of those services. Without the handicapping condition, flexibility of standards on behalf of the child would be viewed as compromising the system, rather than the magnanimous choice of an enlightened system. The handicap provides the credibility to allow for flexibility. Without it, the standards may be manipulated for individual purposes, with the result that the standards are rendered meaningless.

Determination of whether or not the student should take the minimum competency test and how it should be administerd should be part of the IEP meeting and the IEP document itself. This can become another way in which the system can demonstrate its willingness to tailor itself to the individual needs of children. (For an excellent dis-

cussion of testing options for handicapped, see "Individual-
izing Minimum Competency Testing" by Ellen B. Gillespie,
Journal of Learning Disabilities, Nov., 1983, Vol. 16,
No. 9.)

INDIVIDUALIZING MINIMUM COMPETENCY TESTING FOR LEARNING-DISABLED STUDENTS

Ellen B. Gillespie, PhD
in consultation with
Laurence M. Lieberman, EdD
Associate Editor

With almost 40 states currently developing or implementing some form of minimum competency testing (MCT), the issues involved in including special education students in these testing programs have received a great deal of attention. Most of the articles addressing this area have focused on the identification of problem areas and possible infringements on students' rights. Few have described strategies and options for individualizing the decision-making process for testing learning-disabled students.

During the 1981–82 school year, the Louisiana State Department of Education began implementing one of the most ambitious testing programs in the country. Beginning with the second grade, a test of basic skills mastery will be administered to students, with a grade level added each year until all grade 2 through 12 students are tested annually. Scores on the state test are the principal criteria for grade-to-grade promotion. Each local education agency submits a Pupil Progression Plan outlining how Basic Skills Test scores and other factors (such as attendance, teacher observation, and local test scores) will be considered for promotion. Students who do not achieve the required minimum scores will receive state-funded compensatory/remedial education.

Like most educational programs developed for regular education, the problems of "fitting" special education students in the Basic Skills Test policies and procedures have been complex. Some state and local minimum competency testing programs have excluded special education students (or students with certain special education classifications); the policies and procedures for the Louisiana Basic Skills Test emphasize individual needs, regardless of special education classification.

Which Students Should Be Tested?

One of the most common dilemmas concerning MCT and special education students has been determining which students to test. Obviously, if students have not covered the skills to be tested, the issue of curriculum validity arises. An examination of the content of the student's educational program is needed to determine what skills are being addressed.

The individualized education program (IEP) committee decides whether a learning-disabled (or any special education) student will take the Louisiana Basic Skills Test. This decision is based on whether the IEP indicates that the student is addressing the state-adopted minimum skills in reading and mathematics. A student need not be on grade level, but simply should be working on some of these skills. If the student is addressing state minimum skills, his placement is designated as "specially designed regular instruction." Students in specially designed regular instruction participate in the Basic Skills Test and work toward a regular high-school diploma. The 1982 Grade 2 test was administered to 1,197 learning-disabled students in the state who were enrolled in specially designed regular instruction.

The IEP places students not addressing the state minimum skills in their educational programs in an "alternative to regular placement." These students address separate minimum standards developed by special educators, and do not take the Basic Skills Test. Students in alternative to regular placement work toward a Certificate of Achievement, rather than a high-school diploma. A total of 477 learning-disabled students in the state were coded as alternative students for the 1982 Grade 2 test.

Two advantages of this dual approach to curriculum and testing are (1) the extension of the accountability concept to all students, not just those studying reading and math, and (2) the development of a meaningful alternative to the regular diploma. The Certificate of Achievement will not be awarded simply on the basis of years enrolled in school, but will indicate mastery of an individually designed program of education.

Designation of a student as placed in specially designed regular instruction or alternative to regular placement is made on the IEP form. Students in alternative to regular placement must have a parent's signature on the form, thus indicating that the parent understand [sic] that this placement could mean, his child will not receive a regular high-school diploma. The placement decision is made at least annually and designation as "specially designed regular instruction" or as "alternative to regular placement" may be changed at that time. These procedures are meant to allow as many special education students to be tested as possible, but to prevent unnecessary or inappropriate testing.

How Can Tests Be Modified?
The use of test modifications is another concern in implementing a testing program. While test modifications should not give an unfair advantage to special education students, it is apparent that a student with a limited attention span may need several short testing sessions, or that a student with poor fine-motor skills may need help completing a machine-scorable answer sheet. The key to effective test modifications is accommodation for a student's disability without invalidating the test as a measure of basic skills.

Currently, the Louisiana State Department of Education allows the use of nine format or procedural modifications on the Basic Skills Test. The modifications include:

o   Braille test edition

- o   Large-print edition (The large print edition is a photo-enlarged copy printed on $8\frac{1}{2}$ by 11" paper.)
- o   Answers recorded by the test administrator (If a student is unable to mark the answers, provisions must be made for a test administrator to record the student's answers.)
- o   Extended time (Although the Basic Skills Test is not a timed test, some students may need considerable alteration of the testing schedule. It may be determined appropriate to administer the test over several days in a series of short sessions.)
- o   Sign language
- o   Transferred answers (In some cases, a student may mark the test booklet and a test administrator must transfer the student's answers to an answer sheet.)
- o   Individual or small group test administration
- o   Math test read aloud (Students who need such a modification may have the math section, but not the language arts section, read to them.)

Louisiana's policy related to modifications is unique in that Basic Skills Test modifications are not limited to students with particular exceptionalities, but may be used by any special education student as needed. Test modifications are selected in the IEP meeting, thus allowing for input from parents, teachers, and other school staff members. During the first year of the testing program (the 1982 Grade 2 Basic Skills Test), 44% of the learning-disabled students had test directions repeated, 40% took the test in an individual- or small-group administration, and 30% were given extended time. The math test was read to 15% of the learning-disabled students taking the test, and other modifications were used less frequently.

Who Should Administer The Test?

Even the issue of selecting a test administrator is complicated for special education students. Learning–disabled students, who are likely to have regular and special education teachers, could be tested in a resource room or in the regular classroom. The use of some test modifications in a regular class setting could be stigmatizing, however, or might even be impossible to use.

Rather than establishing guidelines for the test administrators, the Louisiana State Department of Education chose an individualized approach for this issue. The choice of test administrator for students taking the Basic Skills Test is left to the school. Paraprofessionals cannot serve as test administrators, however, and modifications should be considered in choosing the test setting.

What Happens to Test Scores?

Reporting test scores for individual students is no more complicated for special education students than for others. However, when scores are combined at the school or local district level, problems arise. In situations in which the news media make comparisons (among school districts), school administrators could view the option of combining special education students' scores with others negatively. This could result in local districts excluding learning disabled and other special education students from testing to avoid adverse affects on district average scores. In Louisiana, the Basic Skills Test scores of special education students are reported separately by exceptionality in school, local district, and state reports. Only the scores of gifted/talented, speech-impaired, and hospital/ homebound students are combined with those of regular education. This means of reporting assures that special education test results are available, but that the politics of score reporting do not result in the exclusion of some students.

The Louisiana Basic Skills Test is only one example of a minimum competency testing program including special education students. The keys to implementation of the program are individualization, consideration of each child's educational program and testing needs, and emphasis on shared decision-making. Although a high proportion of learning-disabled students (68% in language arts and 84% in mathematics) passed the 1982 Grade 2 Basic Skills Test, field testing indicates that the increasing complexity of skills at higher grade levels will result in lower proportions of learning-disabled students passing. As the testing program is implemented through the grades, it will become increasingly important that a variety of options are available. As with all educational programs, test planning must be considered in light of students who have a wide range of abilities. The outcome of this emphasis on individualization wil be the development of testing programs that are fair for all students involved.

Dr. Gillespie is an education specialist for the state of Louisiana's Bureau of Evaluation.
Address: Bureau of Evaluation
            Louisiana State Department of Education
            P.O. Box 44064
            Baton Rouge, LA 70804

CONCLUSION

When a handicapped child spends part of his school day in regular classrooms, and as the result of his handicap, fails in those classrooms, there is only one program option: full time placement outside those regular classrooms. Therefore, when a student is brought before the problem solving team, examined by the pre-referral committee, his teacher is provided support and consultation, the student is declared handicapped, and an IEP is written that reflects partial placement in a regular classroom, there is no option to fail. That is, there is no option to fail unless the school system is prepared to place the child in a self-contained special class. Attempts to provide an appropriate education in regular class settings through the problem solving team, pre-referral committee, and consultation must succeed if regular class placement for handicapped children is to have any validity.

There are significant numbers of children who are not handicapped, yet also struggling and in fact, failing in school. They need help in order to be successful in regular education. Most of the propositions presented in this guide have direct applicability to this group. Many of these children are being helped through special education services, even though they are not handicapped in a broader, traditional sense. Sometimes special education is the only mechanism available to provide this help and in this case, should provide services.

Often, there are numerous other regular education program possiblities that are not employed or underemployed on behalf of children with regular education problems. In this case, special education should not be the first priority, but the last resort.

If regular educators want answers to their problems, they must look inside themselves. If they want ideas, let them look inside this guide.

OTHER PUBLICATIONS BY DR. LIEBERMAN

Lieberman, L. M. Mainstreaming: Strategy or Tragedy? Learning Disabilities: An Audio Journal for Continuing Education, October, 1979, Vol. 3, No. 10.

Lieberman, L. M. The Implications of Noncategorical Special Education. Journal of Learning Disabilities, February, 1980, Vol. 13, No. 2.

Lieberman, L. M. Territoriality - Who Does What To Whom? Journal of Learning Disabilities, March, 1980, Vol. 13, No. 3.

Lieberman, L. M. A Decision-Making Model for In-Grade Retention (Non-Promotion). Journal of Learning Disabilities, May, 1980, Vol. 13, No. 5.

Lieberman, L. M. Parents . . . Where Are You? Perceptions, Sept., 1980, Vol. 3, No. 3.

Lieberman, L. M. Mainstreaming for the Eighties. Academic Therapy, Sept., 1980, Vol. 16, No. 1.

Lieberman, L. M. The Special Education Consultant and the Federal Dollar. Journal of Learning Disabilities, June/July, 1981, Vol. 14, No. 6.

Lieberman, L. M. The LD Adolescent . . . When Do You Stop? Journal of Learning Disabilities, August/September, 1981, Vol. 14, No. 7.

Lieberman, L. M. Special Education's Perilous Path. Academic Therapy, Sept., 1981, Vol. 17, No. 1.

Lieberman, L. M. Two IEP Dilemmas. Journal of Learning Disabilities, October, 1981, Vol. 14, No. 8.

Lieberman, L. M. A Significant Destructive Attitude. Journal of Learning Disabilities, November, 1981, Vol. 14, No. 9.

Lieberman, L. M. The Nightmare of Scheduling. Journal of Learning Disabilities, January, 1982, Vol. 15, No. 1.

Lieberman, L. M. and McNeil, D. Evaluating Special Education Programs. Journal of Learning Disabilities, February, 1982, Vol. 15, No. 2.

Lieberman, L. M. Educational Assessment. Journal of Learning Disabilities, March, 1982, Vol. 15, No. 3.

Lieberman, L. M. On the Topic of Behavior Management. Journal of Learning Disabilities, April, 1982, Vol. 15, No. 4.

Lieberman, L. M. The Regular Classroom Environment. Journal of Learning Disabilities, May, 1982, Vol. 15, No. 5.

Lieberman, L. M. Grades. Journal of Learning Disabilities, June/July, 1982, Vol. 15, No. 6.

Lieberman, L. M. Special Education's Safety Net. Journal of Learning Disabilities, August/September, 1982, Vol. 15, No. 7.

Lieberman, L. M. Learning Principles and Teaching Models. Journal of Learning Disabilities, October, 1982, Vol. 15, No. 8.

Lieberman, L. M. Itard: The Great Problem Solver. Journal of Learning Disabilities, November, 1982, Vol. 15, No. 9.

Lieberman, L. M. On Aggressiveness. Journal of Learning Disabilities, January, 1983, Vol. 16, No. 1.

Lieberman, L. M. Giving Permission. Journal of Learning Disabilities, February, 1983, Vol. 16, No. 2.

Lieberman, L. M. In Praise of Normalcy. Journal of Learning Disabilities, April, 1983, Vol. 16, No. 4.

Lieberman, L. M. What if . . . ? Journal of Learning Disabilities, June/July, 1983, Vol. 16, No. 6.

Lieberman, L. M. The Homework Solution. Journal of Learning Disabilities, August/September, 1983, Vol. 16, No. 7.

Lieberman, L. M. Can't vs. Won't: The Razor's Edge. Journal of Learning Disabilities, October, 1983, Vol. 16, No. 8.

Lieberman, L. M. The Day the Informality Died. Journal of Learning Disabilities, December, 1983, Vol. 16, No. 10.

Lieberman, L. M. Specific Problems Spawn Spin-Off Solutions. Journal of Learning Disabilities, January, 1984, Vol. 17. No. 1.

Lieberman, L. M. Visual Perception versus Visual Function. Journal of Learning Disabilities, March, 1984, Vol. 17, No. 3.

Lieberman, L. M. Euphemisms. Journal of Learning Disabilities, May, 1984, Vol. 17, No. 5.

Lieberman, L. M. Child Centeredness. Journal of Learning Disabilities, August/September, 1984, Vol. 17, No. 7.